bearing
the
standard

*a rallying cry to
uphold the Scriptures*

bearing
the standard

a rallying cry to
uphold the Scriptures

kevin geoffrey & c. h. mackintosh

a ministry of perfect word ministries

A ministry of Perfect Word Ministries

PO Box 82954 • Phoenix, AZ 85071
www.perfect-word.org
1-888-321-PWMI

ISBN #: 978-0-9837263-2-6

Library of Congress Control Number: 2013907360

Printed in the United States of America

To Esther
For walking with me

CONTENTS

Preface ix

The Bible: Its Sufficiency and Supremacy (C. H. Mackintosh) 1

Bearing the Standard of Scripture (Kevin Geoffrey) 17

PART ONE: NO OTHER STANDARD 19

Something to See **22**

Fixing our Eyes **24**

Identifying Hostile Influences **27**

Tradition: Scripture's Fallible Interpreter **29**

Expediency: Shortcutting Scripture for the Sake of Doing "Good" **33**

Rationalism: The Supremacy of Man's Reason **37**

Losing Sight of the Standard **42**

PART TWO: TESTING OUR AIM 45

The Influence of Tradition **51**

When Tradition Fails **53**

Sidestepping Scripture **55**

Chasing and Defending Shadows **58**

The Practical Effects of Tradition **61**

The Influence of Expediency **65**

Doing All the Good We Can **67**

The Path of Obedience **70**

When Shortcuts Become Sidetracks **73**

The Practical Effects of Expediency **78**

The Influence of Rationalism **81**

A Way That Seems Right **84**

Branding Scripture as "Defective" **90**

Denying the Authority of Scripture **94**

The Practical Effects of Rationalism **100**

PART THREE: SUFFICIENT AND SUPREME 105

The Reality of Our Vulnerability **109**

Unconditional Obedience **112**

The Narrow Path **115**

Time to Choose **121**

Raising the Standard **127**

A Call to Action **133**

Arise, and Go Forth! **145**

Join the Cause 151

References 159

About the Authors 163

PREFACE

I HAD NEVER BEFORE HEARD of C. H. Mackintosh when I recently happened upon a reproduction of his pamphlet, *The Bible: Its Sufficiency and Supremacy.* I had only read a few lines of it before needing to stop and begin again, this time reading aloud to Esther and the boys. As she and I wept—hearing the travail of our hearts captured so succinctly and eloquently in the words of an obscure, nineteenth-century, Irish preacher—we suddenly felt a little less alone in our seemingly solitary and hopeless campaign to exhort the contemporary Body of Messiah to bear the standard of Scripture.

Over the course of that initial reading, I was immediately struck by Mackintosh's clarity of thought, conviction of conscience, and kindred spirit. But what ultimately moved me to tears was the realization that he had sounded his clarion warning *more than a hundred and fifty years past.* He saw then, in germinating form, Messiah's gravely infirmed Body of *today*: infected by and succumbing to the philosophies and compromises of man; carelessly permitting the erosion of Scripture as the bedrock of our faith. It didn't take long for me to recognize the providence of having intersected with Mackintosh's essay. The heart of this message must be made an unavoidable issue in every generation—we need to courageously promote the Scriptures and combat its assailants, now more than ever.

The ravenous manner in which we indiscriminately consume information and opinions suggests that what Mackintosh maintains is true: be it politics or academia, the media and entertainment, the bowels of an egocentric internet, or the high places of spiritual celebrity, every surrounding force is bent on persuading us that "we need other guidance than that which [the Bible's] precious pages supply." Rather than each one of us taking personal responsibility to turn to God and His Word for *every* answer and *every* directive, we instead deceive ourselves and default to those deemed more experienced, more educated, or more enlightened. Whether by other men's design or our own self-inflicted disability, the light of Scripture grows ever dimmer in our collective eyes.

Mackintosh's point—and the purpose of this expanded work—is to assert and champion the single fundamental belief that "men must either deny that the Bible is the Word of God, or admit its sufficiency and supremacy." There is no middle ground. The Scriptures must be either complete and outright foolishness, or the unrivaled pronouncement of God's revealed wisdom and truth. As disciples of Messiah, walking daily in the Spirit, we have no choice but to completely abandon our half-hearted, compartmentalized faith, and confess that God alone has full and utter authority. Our only valid response to the sufficiency and supremacy of Scripture is absolute submission and immediate obedience.

It is to this most awesome end that we humbly and soberly send forth the call to uphold the Scriptures. I would be remiss in failing to make clear, however, that while the entirety of this book assumes the belief that the Scriptures are the solely authoritative, written revelation of God's perfect Word, it is not my goal here to defend such an essential belief (indeed, I have written about this subject at length elsewhere). Rather, the message of *Bearing the Standard* simply rests on the glorious, foundational truth that "every Scripture"—from Genesis to Revelation—"*is* God-breathed" (2 Timothy 3:16);

that God inspired men to infallibly and inerrantly encode His divine Word into the stuff of human language and thought.

It is also worthwhile to mention that I am writing here to a broader audience than I am usually accustomed. Much of what I have written and taught over the last fifteen years has been aimed primarily at those known as Messianic Jews; that is, Jewish believers in Jesus—among whom I am also counted. As such, it is my usual practice to refer to the Messiah as *Yeshua* (which, in Hebrew, means "salvation," see Matthew 1:21), and this is the name that I use throughout the book. You will also notice my occasional use of other Hebrew words and phrases, though, for the sake of my Christian brothers and sisters, I have tried to keep such instances to a minimum. To be sure, my frame of reference and peculiar expression of faith are couched in my identity as a Jew, but that same identity *in Messiah* also fuels my passion for proclaiming the perfection of the Word, and the message of its sufficiency and supremacy for all.

My fellow-servant of Messiah, the overflow of faithlessness abounds in this lost generation. Yet even as the threadbare fabric of society's morals hastens to unravel—even as humanity gives way to unthinkable depravities of every kind—there remains but one crucial issue for this and every age: will we surrender our wills and trust our lives *solely* to the Word of God? This is the question that I pray will arrest you as you consider *The Bible: Its Sufficiency and Supremacy* (which I have reproduced below with only minor revisions for clarity) and my following exploration in *Bearing the Standard of Scripture*. Though such discussion marks merely the beginning of a critical conversation, we must nevertheless commit ourselves in advance to reaching the only legitimate conclusion: the fostering of a generation who will disregard all other influences, and pledge its life—without compromise—to bearing the standard of Scripture.

For the sake of the Messiah,

Kevin Geoffrey
December 5, 2012

THE BIBLE:
ITS SUFFICIENCY
AND SUPREMACY

BY C. H. MACKINTOSH

S OME, WE ARE AWARE, would gladly persuade us that things are so totally changed since the Bible was penned, that we need other guidance than that which its precious pages supply. They tell us that society is not what it was; that the human race has made progress; that there has been such a development of the powers of nature, the resources of science, and the applications of philosophy, that to maintain the sufficiency and supremacy of the Bible, at such a point in the world's history as the nineteenth century of the Christian era, can only be regarded as childishness, ignorance, or imbecility.

Now, the men that tell us these things may be very clever and very learned; but we have no hesitation whatever in telling them that, in this matter, "they do greatly err, not knowing the Scriptures, nor the power of God." We certainly do desire to render all due respect to learning, genius, and talent, whenever we find them in their right place, and at their proper work; but when we find them lifting their proud heads above the Word of God; when we find them sitting in judgement, and hurling an insult upon that peerless revelation, we feel that we owe them no respect whatever; yea, we treat them as so many agents of the devil, in his efforts to shake those eternal pillars on which the faith of God's people has ever rested. We cannot listen for a moment to men, however profound in their reading and thinking, who dare to treat God's book as though it were man's book, and speak of those pages that were penned by the Allwise, Almighty, and Eternal God, as though they were the production of a shallow and short-sighted mortal.

It is important that the reader should see clearly that men must either deny that the Bible is the Word of God, or admit its sufficiency and supremacy in all ages, and in all countries—in all stages and conditions of the human race. Grant us but this, that God has written a book for man's guidance, and we argue that that book must be amply sufficient for man, no matter when, where, or how we find him. "All scripture is given by inspiration of God… that the man of God may be *perfect* (ἄρτιος), *thoroughly furnished* unto *all* good works" (2 Tim. 3:16-17). This, surely, is enough. To be perfect and thoroughly furnished, necessarily renders a man independent of all the boasted powers (falsely so called) of science and philosophy.

We are quite aware that, in writing thus, we expose ourselves to the sneer of the learned rationalist, and the polished and cultivated philosopher. But we are not very careful about this. We greatly admire the answer of a pious, but, no doubt, very ignorant woman to some very learned man who was endeavouring to show her that the inspired writer had made a mistake in asserting that Jonah was in the whale's belly. He assured her that such a thing could not possibly be, inasmuch that the natural history of the whale proved it could not swallow anything so large.

"Well," said the poor woman, "I do not know much about natural history; but this I know, that if the Bible were to tell me that Jonah swallowed the whale, I would believe it."

Now, it is quite possible many would pronounce this poor woman to have been under the influence of ignorance and blind gullibility; but, for our part, we should rather be the ignorant woman, confiding in God's Word, than the learned rationalist trying to pick holes in it. We have no doubt as to who was in the safer position.

But, let it not be supposed that we prefer ignorance to learning. Let none imagine that we despise the discoveries of science, or treat with contempt the achievements of sound philosophy. Far from it. We honour them highly in their proper sphere. We could not say how much we prize the labours of those learned men who have consecrated their energies to the work of clearing the sacred text of the various errors and corruptions which, from age to age, had crept into it, through the carelessness or infirmity of copyists, taken advantage of by a crafty and malignant foe. Every effort put forth to preserve, to unfold, to illustrate, and to enforce the precious truth of Scripture, we most highly esteem; but, on the other hand, when we find men making use of their learning, their science, and their philosophy, for the purpose of undermining the sacred fortress of divine revelation, we deem it our duty, to raise our voice, in the clearest and strongest way, against them, and to warn the reader, most solemnly, against their exceedingly harmful influence.

We believe that the Bible, as written in the original Hebrew and Greek languages, is the very word of the only wise and the only true God, with whom one day is as a thousand years, and a thousand years as one day, who saw the end from the beginning, and not only the end, but every stage of the way. We therefore hold it to be nothing short of positive blasphemy to assert that we have arrived at a stage of our career in which the Bible is not sufficient, or that we are compelled to travel outside its covers to find ample guidance and instruction for the present moment, and for every moment of our earthly pilgrimage. The Bible is a perfect chart, in which every necessity of the Christian mariner has been anticipated. Every rock, every sand-bank, every reef, every strand, every island, has been carefully noted down. All the need of the Church of God, its members, and its ministers, has been most fully provided for. How could it be otherwise if we admit the Bible to be the Word of God? Could the mind of God have devised, or His finger sketched an imperfect chart? Impossible. We must either deny the divinity or admit the sufficiency of *The Book*. We are absolutely shut up to this alternative. There is not so much as a single point between these two positions. If the book is incomplete, it cannot be of God; if it be of God, it must be perfect. But if we are compelled to commit ourselves to other sources for guidance and instruction, as to the path of the Church of God, its members or its ministers, then is the Bible incomplete, and being such, it cannot be of God at all.

What then are we to do? Whither can we commit ourselves? If the Bible be not a divine and therefore all-sufficient guide-book, what remains? Some will tell us to have recourse to **tradition**. Alas! what a miserable guide. No sooner have we launched out into the wide field of tradition than our ears are assailed by ten thousand strange and conflicting sounds. We meet, it may be, with a tradition which seems very authentic, very venerable, well worthy of respect and confidence, and we commit ourselves to its guidance; but, directly we have done so, another tradition crosses our path, putting forth quite as strong claims on our confidence, and leading us in quite an opposite direction. Thus it is with tradition. The mind is bewildered, and one is reminded of the assembly at Ephesus, concerning which we read that, "Some cried one thing, and some another; for the assembly was confused." The fact is, we want a perfect standard, and this can only be found in a divine revelation, which, as we believe, is to be found within the covers of our most precious Bible. What a treasure! How we should bless God for it! How we should praise His name for His mercy in that He hath not left His Church dependent upon the deceptive hope of human tradition, but upon the steady light of divine revelation! We do not want tradition to assist revelation, but we use revelation as the test of tradition. We should just as soon think of bringing out a rush-light to assist the sun's meridian beams, as of calling in human tradition to aid divine revelation.

But there is another very ensnaring and dangerous resource presented by the enemy of the Bible, and alas! accepted by too many of the people of God, and that is **expediency**, or the very attractive plea of doing all the good we can, without due attention to the way in which that good is done. The tree of expediency is a wide-spreading one, and yields most tempting clusters. But remember, its clusters will prove bitter as wormwood in the end. It is, no doubt, well to do all the good we can; but let us look well to the way in which we do it. Let us not deceive ourselves by the vain imagination that God will ever accept of services based upon positive disobedience to His Word. "It is a gift," said the elders, as they boldly walked over the plain commandment of God, as if He would be pleased with a gift presented on such a principle. There is an intimate connection between the ancient "corban" and the modern "expediency," for "there is nothing new under the sun." The solemn responsibility of obeying the Word of God was got rid of under the plausible pretext of "corban," or "it is a gift" (Mark 7:7-13).

Thus it was of old. The "corban" of the ancients justified, or sought to justify, many a bold transgression of the law of God; and the "expediency" of our times allures many to outstep the boundary line laid down by divine revelation.

Now, we quite admit that expediency holds out most attractive inducements. It does seem so very delightful to be doing a great deal of good, to be gaining the ends of a large-hearted benevolence, to be reaching tangible results. It would not be an easy matter duly to estimate the ensnaring influences of such objects, or the immense difficulty of throwing them overboard. Have we never been tempted as we stood upon the narrow path of obedience, and looked forth upon the golden fields of expediency lying on either side, to exclaim, "Alas! I am sacrificing my usefulness for an idea"? Doubtless; but then what if it should turn out that we have the very same foundation for that "idea" as for the fundamental doctrines of salvation? The question is, What is the idea? Is it founded upon "Thus saith the Lord"? If so, let us tenaciously hold by it, though ten thousand advocates of expediency were hurling at us the grievous charge of narrow-mindedness.

There is immense power in Samuel's brief but pointed reply to Saul, "Hath the Lord as great delight in burnt offerings and sacrifices as in obeying the voice of the Lord! Behold, to obey is better than sacrifice, and to hearken than the fat of rams" (1 Sam. 15:22). Saul's word was *"Sacrifice."* Samuel's word was *"Obedience."* No doubt the bleating of the sheep and the lowing of the oxen were most exciting. They would be looked upon as substantial proofs that something was being done; while on the other hand, the path of obedience seemed narrow, silent, lonely, and fruitless. But oh! those pungent words of Samuel! *"to obey is better than sacrifice."* What a triumphant answer to the most eloquent advocates of expediency! They are most conclusive—most commanding words. They teach us that it is better, if it must be so, to stand, like a marble statue, on the pathway of obedience, than to reach the most desirable ends by transgressing a plain precept of the Word of God.

But let none suppose that one must be like a statue on the path of obedience. Far from it. There are rare and precious services to be rendered by the obedient one—services which can only be rendered by such, and which owe all their preciousness to their being the fruit of simple obedience. True, they may not find a place in the public record of man's bustling activity; but they are recorded on high, and they will be published at the right time. As a dear friend has often said to us, "Heaven will be the safest and happiest place to hear all about our work down here." May we remember this, and pursue our way, in all simplicity, looking to Christ for guidance, power, and blessing. May His smile be enough for us. May we not be found looking sideways to catch the approving look of a poor mortal whose breath is in his nostrils, nor sigh to find our names amid the glittering record of the great men of the age. The servant of Christ should look far beyond all such things. The grand business of the servant is to obey. His object should not be to do a great deal, but simply to do what he is told. This makes all plain; and, moreover, it will make the Bible precious as the depository of the Master's will, to which he must continually commit himself to know what he is to do, and how he is to do it. Neither tradition nor expediency will do for the servant of Christ. The all-important inquiry is, "What saith the Scriptures."

This settles everything. From the decision of the Word of God there must be no appeal. When God speaks, man must bow. It is not by any means a question of obstinate adherence to a man's own notions. Quite the opposite. It is a reverent adherence to the Word of God. Let the reader distinctly mark this. It often happens that, when one is determined, through grace, to abide by Scripture, he will be pronounced dogmatic, intolerant and dictatorial; and, no doubt, one has to watch over his temper, spirit, and style, even when seeking to abide by the Word of God. But, be it well remembered, obedience to Christ's commandments is the very opposite of dictatorship, dogmatism, and intolerance. It is not a little strange that when a man tamely consents to place his conscience in the keeping of his fellow, and to bow down his understanding to the opinions of men, he is considered meek, modest, and liberal; but let him reverently bow to the authority of the holy Scripture, and he will be looked upon as self-confident, dogmatic, and narrow-minded. Be it so. The time is rapidly approaching when obedience shall be called by its right name, and meet its recognition and reward. For that moment the faithful must be content to wait, and while waiting for it, be satisfied to let men call them whatever they please. "The Lord knoweth the thoughts of man, that they are vanity."

But we must draw to a close, and would merely add, in conclusion, that there is a third hostile influence against which the lover of the Bible will have to watch, and that is **rationalism**—or the supremacy of man's reason. The faithful disciple of the Word of God will have to withstand this audacious intruder, with the most unflinching decision. It presumes to sit in judgment upon the Word of God—to decide upon what is and what is not worthy of God—to prescribe boundaries to inspiration. Instead of humbly bowing to the authority of Scripture, which continually soars into a region where poor blind reason can never follow, it proudly seeks to drag Scripture down to its own level. If the Bible puts forth anything which, in the smallest degree, clashes with the conclusions of rationalism, then there must be some flaw. God is shut out of His own book if He says anything which poor, blind, perverted reason cannot reconcile with her own conclusions—which conclusions, be it observed, are not infrequently the grossest absurdities.

Nor is this all. Rationalism deprives us of the only perfect standard of truth, and conducts us into a region of the most dreary uncertainty. It seeks to undermine the authority of a Book in which we can believe everything, and carries us into a field of speculation in which we can be sure of nothing. Under the dominion of rationalism the soul is like a vessel broken from its safe moorings in the haven of divine revelation, to be tossed like a cork upon the wild watery waste of universal scepticism.

Now we do not expect to convince a thorough rationalist, even if such a one should condescend to scan our unpretending pages, which is most unlikely. Neither could we expect to gain over to our way of thinking the decided advocate of expediency, or the ardent admirer of tradition. We have neither the competency, the leisure, nor the space, to enter upon such a line of argument as would be required were we seeking to gain such ends as these. But we are most anxious that the Christian reader should rise up from the perusal of this volume with a deepened sense of the preciousness of his Bible. We earnestly desire that the words, *"The Bible: its sufficiency and supremacy,"* should be engraved, in deep and broad characters, upon the tablet of the reader's heart.

We feel that we have a solemn duty to perform, at a moment like the present, in which superstition, expediency, and rationalism are all at work, as so many agents of the devil, in his efforts to sap the foundations of our holy faith. We owe it to that blessed volume of inspiration, from which we have drunk the streams of life and peace, to bear our feeble testimony to the divinity of its every page—to give expression, in this permanent form, to our profound reverence for its authority, and our conviction of its divine sufficiency for every need, whether of the believer individually, or the church collectively.

We press upon our readers earnestly to set a higher value than ever upon the Holy Scriptures, and to warn them, in most urgent terms, against every influence, whether of tradition, expediency, or rationalism, which might tend to shake their confidence in those heavenly oracles. There is a spirit abroad, and there are principles at work, which make it imperative upon us to keep close to Scripture—to treasure it in our hearts—and to submit to its holy authority.

May God the Spirit, the Author of the Bible, produce, in the writer and reader of these lines, a more ardent love for that Bible! May He enlarge our experience and acquaintance with its contents, and lead us into more complete subjection to its teachings in all things, that God may be more glorified in us through Jesus Christ our Lord. Amen.

BEARING
THE STANDARD
OF SCRIPTURE

BY KEVIN GEOFFREY

PART ONE

No Other Standard

I SRAEL HAD BEEN MIRACULOUSLY delivered from centuries of Egyptian slavery. No one could have known she would soon find herself wandering the desert of punishment—awaiting the slow death of her faithless and eldest generation. At God's hand, Israel experienced both grave loss and monumental triumph; yet despite His abundant presence and provision, Israel's trust of God was severely lacking. With *barely six months remaining* in their desert exile, the people of Israel could still speak the unthinkable: *"Why have you brought us up out of Egypt to die in a wilderness?"* (Numbers 21:5). God was invisible and unreal to Israel... after forty long years, they simply did not believe.

With Israel blinded to their ever-present salvation, God then unleashed upon the people a danger of the desert—reminding them just Who had the power to hold it back. In answer to the defining, forty-year-old lesson which Israel had failed to learn, God gave His condemning response:

> And ADONAI (the LORD) sent among the people
> the burning serpents, and they bit the people, and
> many people of Israel died. בְּמִדְבַּר NUMBERS 21:6

As the people recoiled from their chastisement, they repented to God in their usual, short-lived desperation. Even so, Adonai once again brought salvation to Israel—but this time, by *lifting up a standard* before them. Israel would receive deliverance and life anew because the invisible God gave them something to see.

> And Adonai said to Moses, "Make for you a burning *serpent*, and **set it on a standard**; and it will be, everyone who is bitten and has seen it—he has lived." And Moses made a serpent of brass, and **set it on the standard**, and it was, if the serpent bit any man, and he looked expectingly to the serpent of brass—he has lived. בְּמִדְבַּר Numbers 21:8-9

Anyone who "looked expectingly" toward the standard: *he has lived.*

SOMETHING TO SEE

Had you or I been one of those poor, afflicted souls, what sight would our eyes have seen? A magical, bronze snake tacked atop a pole? Or the faithful, creative, steadfast salvation of the One True and Living God?

By lifting up a standard—setting something up high above for all to see—Moses provided a *tangible* rallying point, a *perceptible* place of focus, to draw the peoples' attention and hearts toward the Source of their deliverance. The upholding of God's *standard* made God *Him-*

self visible and real to the people—as they looked expectingly toward the upraised standard, they experienced the restoration and revival of their lives.

Because the mind of man so quickly forgets God (or chooses to ignore Him), and our trust so easily wanes, God establishes His standard—lifts something up high for us to see—that He might increase our faith, and we might believe. And this is why,

> ...as Moses lifted up the serpent in the desert, so **it is necessary for the Son of Man to be lifted up**, [so] that everyone who is believing in Him may have life age-enduring. For God so loved the world, that His Son—the only begotten—He gave... יוֹחָנָן JOHN 3:14-16A

The Master Yeshua (Jesus) has been lifted up for us (cf. Isaiah 11:10)—to reconcile all people to God, to focus us on His power and love, to draw our attentions and hearts to the only Source of all true redemption and deliverance—for "he who has seen Me has seen the Father" (John 14:9). In Yeshua, God truly gave the world something awesome, amazing, and astounding to see! And yet, the Messiah's dwelling among men would be brief—the habitation of Imanuel ("God with us") would last but a moment—then "the world will see Me no more" (John 14:19).

How, then, would the world profess the One they had not known?

How, *now*, will He become real to us who have never seen?

Though intangible, we may yet run to Him; though imperceptible, still, we perceive. For the Master, too, has *lifted up a standard*—set something up high above for all to see—something that draws us to Him.

> And He said to them, "...it is necessary for **all the things that are written about Me**... to be fulfilled." Then He opened up their understanding to understand **the Scriptures**. LUKE 24:44-45

As we look expectingly toward the upraised standard of Yeshua, we experience the restoration and revival of our lives. By the Spirit of Truth, we know and see the reality of Yeshua when we look faithfully to the standard of Scripture.

FIXING OUR EYES

Since the beginning, *the Word* of God has been continually speaking to all creation (see John 1:1-3; Colossians 1:15-17).

In Yeshua, *the Word* became flesh, to demonstrate and proclaim to us the reality of God.

And in the Scriptures, the encoded archive of *that very same Word*, God continues to speak to us of His reality and truth, so that we in turn may demonstrate and proclaim His salvation to the world.

The Master Yeshua upheld Scripture as a standard, not simply because it *speaks* of Him, but because Scripture itself *is* His very Word. When we read and believe that the Scriptures are true, the reality of God is within reach.

But belief alone is not enough.

Our outward response to God's Word is the *exact measure* of our inner devotion to Him. If we trust God with our lives, then we must permit *His Word alone* to establish our values. If we accept that ADONAI is true, then we must allow *His Word alone* to determine our beliefs. If we rely upon God for His care and protection, then we must invite *His Word alone* to dictate the boundaries of our behavior—from the seed of each instigating thought, to the execution of each resultant action. Walking each day by the Spirit, Scripture *must in every way* be the objective authority and guide by which we find, fix upon, and follow the Master Yeshua… "the author and perfecter of faith" (Hebrews 12:2).

Let us not forget the lesson of Israel's obstructed eyes: Daily, she walked with God, was led by Him, and experienced His presence and provision; yet in so many ways she remained blind to His salvation. And so is it with us today. We walk with God (or so we confess), are led by Him each day (or so we believe), and experience His presence and provision; and still, Yeshua—God's most potent and present reality—remains *unreal* and *invisible* in our everyday lives. God came to us in the flesh, yet we act as if He is *intangible*. His salvation is clearly evident, yet we behave as if He is *imperceptible*. We "hear, but do not understand... see, but do not know" (Isaiah 6:9). Why? Because we have not fixed our eyes on the standard of God's Word and, through that discernible witness, believed that He is real.

This is where bearing the standard of Scripture begins: fixing our eyes on God's Word as the *only acceptable standard* for establishing our values, determining our beliefs, and dictating the boundaries of our behavior. *There is no other standard.* This is the absolute truth to which we must dedicate our lives—the truth we have been selected and placed upon the earth to proclaim: "God! perfect *is* His way; the word of ADONAI is tried [and true]" (Psalm 18:30). Though every force and influence of the world is bent on dissuading us from this truth, we must commit ourselves to *look expectingly* toward the uniquely sufficient and supreme standard of Scripture. For the fulfillment of our destiny as disciples of Messiah, this is the banner we must raise—the standard we have been called forth to uphold—that we may demonstrate and proclaim the reality of Yeshua, so that all who may see... shall live.

IDENTIFYING HOSTILE INFLUENCES

I N *THE BIBLE: ITS SUFFICIENCY* and *Suprem-acy*, C. H. Mackintosh takes his stand for the Scrip-tures, defending the honor of God's holy and perfect Word. Not only does he agree that no other valid stan-dard exists; he also declares that to claim otherwise is an offense against God. Stating that "the Bible, as writ-ten in the original Hebrew and Greek languages, is the very word of the only wise and only true God," Mackintosh then makes his position clear.

> We therefore hold it to be **nothing short of positive blasphemy** to assert that... the Bible is not sufficient, or that we are compelled to travel outside its covers to find ample guidance and instruction....

For Mackintosh, this is *the* fundamental attack on *God's authority:* the belief that we need more than His Word to guide us through life. Such an assertion utterly degrades the Scriptures. When we look to and lift up standards that originate outside of Scripture, we are saying that the Word of God is *insufficient* to teach us what we need to know.

So strongly does Mackintosh hold to this conviction that, in relating the story of the so-called "ignorant" woman who would have believed the Bible to be true even if it said that *Jonah* had swallowed *the whale*, he concluded, "[W]e should rather be the ignorant woman, confiding in God's word, than the learned rationalist trying to pick holes in it." Even our understanding of those things we are *convinced* are reality must be made subject to the authority of the Word of God. We can permit *nothing* to stand against Scripture, share its prominence, or divide our attention. Every word, voice, and idea must be held in no higher regard than Scripture; nor may any be revered as its equal; nor may any be attached to it as its agent, assistant, or interpreter. As "the very word of the only wise and only true God," Scripture—our full and final authority—deserves the highest esteem.

Unfortunately, such submission and honor is rarely granted to Scripture. Even the followers of God often fall prey to what Mackintosh calls "hostile influences." These forces draw our focus away from Scripture and shield its brilliance from our eyes. In light of this problem, Mackintosh points out three specific influences that not only compromise our submission to God's Word, but also weaken our ability to bear the standard of Scripture.

TRADITION: SCRIPTURE'S FALLIBLE INTERPRETER

For many, there is no sacred cow more precious—while for many others, no inheritance more useless—than *tradition*. For its strong proponent, tradition is beyond criticism; for its zealous adversary, it is beyond help. But whether they be family traditions, cultural traditions, or religious traditions, the handing down of beliefs and customs is, in fact, morally neutral. What Mackintosh identifies as "hostile" is not so much the traditions themselves as their *ability to fail* us as a life-guide. He asserts that man-made tradition, as a companion to or replacement for the *unfailing* Scriptures, is misleading by nature. Calling attention to this trait in tradition, he laments:

> [T]radition. Alas! what a miserable guide. No sooner have we launched out into the wide field of tradition than our ears are assailed by ten thousand strange and conflicting sounds. We meet, it may be, with a tradition which seems very authentic, very venerable, well worthy of respect and confidence, and we commit ourselves to its guidance; but, directly we have done so, another tradition crosses our path, putting forth quite as strong claims on our confidence, and leading us in quite an opposite direction. Thus it is with tradition.

Mackintosh likens the broad plains and winding roads of tradition with the confusion at Ephesus: "some were calling out one thing, and some another" (Acts 19:32). We need to realize that tradition, though presenting the face of certainty and stability, is actually wildly erratic. In contrast with Scripture, tradition is *self-determining* and *self-governing*. It can choose to indulge in its slow reconstruction over time, potentially setting itself at odds with its own past and predecessors. What tradition then puts forward as authentic and confidence-worthy may in fact be in conflict with itself. But more than that, it may find itself standing against the only certain and stable guide and instructor we have: the Word of God.

Such conflict is easily seen in the confrontation between Yeshua and the Jewish religious leaders. When
they challenged the Master with: "Why do your disciples sidestep the tradition of the elders?", He immediately retorted, "Why also do you sidestep the command of
God because of your tradition?" (Matthew 15:2-3). The
division couldn't be sharper. On one side are the traditions of men as upheld by the religious multitudes. On
the other side is the Messiah standing alone in defense
of the Word of God. Why the divide? There is no debate as to the traditions' origins (which could be based
in Scripture), their intentions, or even their authenticity, usefulness, or widespread acceptance. No, the issue
is that the traditions—and, perhaps, their evangelists—
have inadvertently usurped *or are deliberately posing as*
God's authority. Indeed, in judgment of such man-made
traditionalism, Yeshua has made His final ruling.

> Isaiah prophesied well concerning you, hypocrites,
> as it has been written, "This people honor Me with
> the lips, but their heart is far from Me; and in vain
> do they worship Me, teaching teachings [that are
> merely the] commands of men." For, having put
> away the command of God, you hold [to] the tra-
> dition of men.... You put away the command of
> God [very] well [so] that you may keep your tra-
> dition.... MARK 7:6-9, QUOTING יְשַׁעְיָהוּ ISAIAH 29:13 (LXX)

The Master teaches us that the traditionalist's first tactic is to evade ("put away" or "sidestep") Scripture—to exploit loopholes in order to keep his traditions intact. But as the "commands of men" collide with the "command of God," the impact reveals the lengths to which we are willing to go. We exert great effort to preserve our practices and maintain the illusion that we are obeying God. But whose voice is really being obeyed? Whose standard is being upheld? This confusion is the inevitable result when we trust in *tradition* as a reliable guide for anything *other than* tradition. As an assistant to Scripture, tradition will eventually lead us astray, and we will find ourselves opposed to the Word of God... chasing and defending shadows. Does any disciple of Messiah knowingly desire such deficient leadership? Certainly not, as Mackintosh attests.

> The fact is, we want a perfect standard, and this can only be found in a divine revelation, which, as we believe, is to be found within the covers of our most precious Bible. What a treasure! How we should bless God for it! How we should praise His name for His mercy in that He [has not left us] dependent upon the deceptive hope of human tradition, but upon the steady light of divine revelation! We do not want tradition to assist revelation [that is, Scripture], but we use revelation as the test of tradition.

The Word of God alone—*revealed* to us in the Scriptures—must be the standard we bear. There is ultimately no hope in the assistance offered by the hazy glow of man's living traditions and subjective interpretations—no matter how ancient, inspired, wise, and authentic they *appear* to be. The enchanting voice of tradition attempts to endear itself to us by praising Scripture for the essential groundwork it lays. But Scripture is not simply foundational and indispensable… it is altogether *sufficient!*

EXPEDIENCY: SHORTCUTTING SCRIPTURE FOR THE SAKE OF DOING "GOOD"

The second influence that Mackintosh considers to be hostile to the Scriptures is *expediency,* or "the very attractive plea of doing all the good we can, without due attention to the way in which that good is done." In other words, we are being *expedient* when we do "good" according to one part of the Scriptures, but take a shortcut through another part of the Scriptures to do it. We compromise and ignore the Word that we find most troubling, so that we may accomplish and celebrate the Word that we find most gratifying. "It does seem so very delightful to be doing a great deal of good," Mackintosh says, "to be gaining the ends of a large-hearted benevolence, to be reaching tangible results." The problem is that any "good"—even Scriptural "good"—done at the expense of God's Word amounts to disobedience.

The Master exposes such expediency in the hearts of the Jewish religious leaders. He confronts them for teaching people to withhold things from their families in order to give more to God. The Master declares,

> ...for Moses said, "HONOR YOUR FATHER AND YOUR MOTHER;" and "HE WHO IS SPEAKING EVIL OF FATHER OR MOTHER —LET HIM DIE THE DEATH;" but you say, "If a man says to [his] father or to [his] mother, 'Whatever you may be profited out of [what is] mine is [already promised as a] קָרְבָּן, *qorban* [corban] (that is, a gift [to God])," then no more do you allow him to do anything for his father or for his mother, [thus] setting aside the word of God... and you do many such things like [this].
>
> MARK 7:10-13, QUOTING שְׁמוֹת EXODUS 20:12, 21:17

קָרְבָּן, *Qorban (corban)*—"a gift"—is an offering to God. It could be anything from meat, to produce, to articles of silver or gold. The Jewish religious leaders were teaching their followers to give offerings to God *at the expense of* their own families. They were teaching people that in order to do "good" (in this case, something "good" for God), it is sometimes necessary to trample the Scriptures (in this case, God's own commands to honor one's parents).

But doesn't Scripture command us to give offerings to God? It does, indeed. And isn't it *good* to give as much as we can to Him? Of course, it is. Then… shouldn't our devotion to God be *more important* than other things, *including the way we treat our family?* Welcome to *expediency!*—"doing all the good we can, without due attention to the way in which that good is done." The Jewish leaders arrived here, as Mackintosh points out, because, "the solemn responsibility of obeying the Word of God was got rid of under the plausible pretext of… 'it is a gift [to God].'" Through their hypocrisy, those leaders fell under the influence of *expediency.* They used the "tangible results" of "a great deal of good" to *justify* setting aside the Scriptures.

King Saul also knew the Word of God, yet *directly disobeyed it through otherwise permitted acts* of devotion. Samuel the prophet brought the Word of God to Saul, telling him to attack the Amalekites (see 1Samuel 15:1-3), which Saul immediately set out to fulfill. But instead of completely destroying the enemy *according to the Word of God*, Saul thought it would be *good* to spare the best animals and use them to make sacrifices to God. When confronted with his disobedience, Saul pointed to his "tangible results" and exclaimed, "But I *did* obey ADONAI!" (see 1Samuel 15:20). To this, Samuel shot back,

> Has ADONAI (the LORD) had [as much] delight in
> burnt-offerings and sacrifices as *in* [your] hearing
> [and obeying] the voice of ADONAI? Look! hear-
> ing [and obeying] is better than sacrifice; to give
> attention [to Him is better] than [the] fat of rams.
>
> שְׁמוּאֵל א 1SAMUEL 15:22

Obeying is better than sacrifice. Had Saul listened to the Word of God, he would have had nothing to show for it but the absence of an enemy. Instead, his heart desired to prove himself to God, and as a result, his "doing all the good" he could became *disobedience!* "Saul's word was *'Sacrifice.'* Samuel's word was *'Obedience,'*" says Mackintosh, offering insight on Saul's inner thoughts. "No doubt the bleating of the sheep and the lowing of the oxen were most exciting. They would be looked upon as substantial proofs that something was being done; while on the other hand, the path of obedience seemed narrow, silent, lonely and fruitless." Saul obeyed his insecurity rather than the Word of God, and then blamed his disobedience on the influence of others (see 1Samuel 15:24). In reality, Saul was under the influence of *expediency:* sacrifice trumps obedience because it offers "substantial proofs" that we are being fruitful and doing *good.*

Expediency undermines the Scriptures because it persuades us to do what we *think* pleases God at the expense of what the Scriptures *tell* us He wants. It gains a foothold when we are unsatisfied with the seemingly "fruitless" path of obedience, and our hearts are enticed by the call of "tangible results" and the affirmation that comes from doing good. Then, our passions and doubts pervert the desire to please God into justification for pleasing ourselves. Finally, we have but to overcome the only remaining obstacle to our self-deception—the perfect Word of God—and disobedience has suddenly delivered us to a most pleasing place. Mackintosh sums it up this way:

> It is, no doubt, well to do all the good we can; but let us look well to the way in which we do it. Let us not deceive ourselves by the vain imagination that God will ever accept of services based upon positive disobedience to His Word.

RATIONALISM: THE SUPREMACY OF MAN'S REASON

Lastly, the third influence that Mackintosh considers hostile to the Scriptures is *rationalism*, or "the supremacy of man's reason." *Rationalism* does not recognize Scripture as man's ultimate authority. Instead, it arrogantly "presumes to sit in judgment upon the Word of God… to prescribe boundaries to [divine] inspiration." In other words, when man's reason and God's Word are in conflict, *rationalism* brands Scripture as *defective*. What is the result? "God is shut out of His own book," snorts Mackintosh, "if He says anything which poor, blind, perverted reason cannot reconcile with her own conclusions." *Rationalism* asserts that man's reason has no equal. It submits itself neither to a supreme Master, nor to the supposedly backward commands of His allegedly archaic Book.

We see *rationalism* on full display in an exchange between Yeshua and the Sadducees. Hoping to discredit Him, they approached the Master to prove *by their reasoning* that there would be no Resurrection ("Rising Again") of the dead (see Matthew 22:23). They presented Yeshua with a scenario in which a woman had been successively married to seven brothers, before each of them had died. They then devised a riddle to demonstrate their superior reasoning and catch Yeshua without an answer. Expecting to stump Him with their genius, they posed the presumptuous question, "[In] the Rising Again, of which of the seven will she be [the] wife…?" (Matthew 22:28). The Sadducees were implying that there is no such thing as the Resurrection, otherwise, the brothers would all be married to the same woman at the same time. *Quod erat demonstrandum*; thus, the argument is proved.

But the reasoning of the Sadducees failed. They did not take into account the reality of the Word of God. Silencing the deafening noise of *rationalism*, the Master countered with His supreme reply.

"**You go astray, not knowing the Scriptures**, nor the power of God! For in the Rising Again [the Resurrection], they do not marry, nor are they given in marriage, but are as Messengers [Angels] of God in Heaven. And concerning the Rising Again from the dead, **did you not read that which was spoken to you by God**, saying, 'I AM THE GOD OF ABRAHAM, AND THE GOD OF ISAAC, AND THE GOD OF JACOB'? God is not a God of dead men, but of living!" And having heard, the crowds were astonished at His teaching.

מַתִּתְיָהוּ MATTHEW 22:29-33, QUOTING שְׁמוֹת Exodus 3:6

Yeshua exposed the error in the Sadducees' reasoning: "You go astray, not knowing the Scriptures." Their line of thinking was flawed because it was in conflict with the Word of God (for example, Deuteronomy 24:3 teaches that a husband's death releases his wife from marriage; cf. Romans 7:2-3 and 1Corinthians 7:39). Indeed, what kind of God would "a God of dead men" be? Rather, by asserting God's present, ongoing status as the God of Abraham, Isaac and Jacob, God Himself declares that the patriarchs—who died—are alive and well; thus, resurrected from the dead!

The Sadducees' lack of humility blinded them to the truth, such that they could not envision the characteristics of the afterlife. They rendered Scripture defective by giving more weight to the reasonings of their minds than the Scriptures they clearly knew ("did you not read…?"). The Master challenged the Sadducees' rationalistic beliefs—astonishing the crowds in the process—by bearing the standard of Scripture.

Ultimately, as Yeshua exclaimed, rationalism denies "the power of God." It does not believe that Scripture has a divine source, and therefore claims the right to ignore and subvert its authority. By challenging the supremacy of Scripture, rationalism tries to make the perfect, unbreakable wisdom of God appear foolish and unreasonable to men's minds.

And we would be foolish and unreasonable indeed to think that, as believers in Yeshua, we are *immune* to the influence of rationalism. The Scriptures are spiritual, but we are of the flesh (see Romans 7:14), and we cannot hope to uphold the Scriptures as long as we remain worldly-minded. Paul warns us that "the natural man does not receive the things of the Spirit of God, for to him they are foolishness" (1Corinthians 2:14). But God's Word is not required to make sense to us in order for it to be true! It is the arrogance of rationalism that holds our minds captive, rendering our actions meaningless, and our thoughts incomplete.

> Let no one deceive himself; if anyone seems to be wise among you in this age—let him become a fool, [so] that he may become wise. For the wisdom of this world is foolishness with God, for it has

been written, "[IT IS GOD] WHO IS CATCH-
ING THE WISE IN THEIR CRAFTINESS;" and
again, "ADONAI (THE LORD) KNOWS THE
REASONINGS OF THE WISE, THAT THEY
ARE VAIN." 1CORINTHIANS 3:18-20, QUOTING אִיּוֹב JOB 5:13
AND תְּהִלִּים PSALMS 94:11

It is not *God's* wisdom that is foolish, but *ours*. Indeed, "Who has measured the Spirit of ADONAI, and,
being His counselor, teaches Him?" (Isaiah 40:13). By
our own self-centered reasoning, we subject God's Word
to personal interpretation (see 2Peter 1:20-21, speaking
specifically about prophecy). And for all our so-called
wisdom and discernment, our lack of restraint leads us
to "twist...[the] Scriptures, to [our] own destruction"
(2Peter 3:16). Rather than depending upon God's Word
for our very lives, we tend to trust in it only to the extent
that it agrees with our opinions. Upon such waves, we
are tossed about... erratic, hopeless, and lost. When we
submit to the influence of rationalism—granting authority to our own reasoning over the Word of God—
we surrender all stability and assurance to the wind.
Mackintosh agrees.

> Rationalism deprives us of the only perfect stan-
> dard of truth, and conducts us into a region of the
> most dreary uncertainty. It seeks to undermine
> the authority of a Book in which we can believe

everything, and carries us into a field of speculation in which we can be sure of nothing.

In what can we place our trust, if not God's Word?
What perfect standard exists, if not the Scriptures?

LOSING SIGHT OF THE STANDARD

As disciples of Messiah, we are under constant as-
sault by forces that are hostile to bearing the standard
of Scripture. By nature, influences such as *tradition*, *expediency*, and *rationalism* attack God's authority, con-
vincing us that we need more than His Word to guide us
through life. *Tradition* tells us that Scripture needs the
assistance of man's customs, interpretations and institutions. *Expediency* tells us that as long as we are doing
"good," we can shortcut and bypass the Scriptures any-
time they get in our way. *Rationalism* tells us that when
man's reason conflicts with God's wisdom, it is Scripture
that is defective. Sometimes we are complicit with this
subversion; but more often, we are oblivious to it. These
influences are so pervasive that we barely know how to
recognize them, much less question them. We have been
under their influence for so long that, as a Body, we are
chronically disoriented.

Once we surrender to misleading influences, we lose
sight of the sufficient and supreme standard we are called
to follow. When we no longer *"look expectingly"* to the

Scriptures as our only acceptable standard, the Master Yeshua vanishes before our eyes, and—immediately— we are lost. How can we raise the banner for others to see, if we ourselves have no idea where to look? How can we demonstrate and proclaim the reality of Yeshua, if we are following a million different counterfeit flags? We cannot. Instead, we have to wake up from our daze and get a fix on our position. We need to test ourselves and evaluate the degree to which we have fallen under hostile influence. Only then may we resist the forces bent on deterring us from the truth... only then can we fix our eyes on God's perfect Word and bear the standard of Scripture.

PART TWO

TESTING OUR AIM

REMEMBER THAT A *STANDARD*—something set up high above for all to see—serves as a tangible rallying point; a perceptible place of focus to which we may *"look expectingly."* As such, the Scriptures are in every way the objective authority and guide by which we as disciples of Messiah are supposed to find, fix upon, and follow the Master Yeshua (Jesus). What has happened, however, is that we have made ourselves vulnerable to hostile influences such as *tradition, expediency, and rationalism,* which draw our focus away from Scripture and shield its brilliance from our eyes. Our cooperation with these forces not only compromises our submission to God's Word, but also weakens our ability to uphold Scripture as our standard. If we truly hope to follow Yeshua, we must fully commit to bearing the standard of Scripture—and it begins with fixing our eyes on God's Word as the only acceptable standard for establishing our values, determining our beliefs, and dictating the boundaries of our behavior.

Let's take some time now to test our aim, and consider what this all means in practical, twenty-first century terms—to evaluate our own real-life effectiveness at bearing the standard of Scripture. Consider these questions for a moment:

Have I been demonstrating in my walk with Yeshua that the Scriptures are the sufficient and supreme guide for my daily life?

Have I truly accepted the Scriptures as the ultimate and final standard for determining my values, beliefs and behavior?

Have I unknowingly fallen victim to certain hostile influences, and been persuaded to undermine, bypass and ignore what the Scriptures say?

To answer these questions and begin our self-examination, we'll take some practical examples from real, everyday life on a subject of relevance to everyone. While we could consider a broad host of topics—such as how we spend our time, use our finances, or treat our families—nearly every human being is highly concerned with one overarching theme: the forming and maintaining of *relationships*; specifically, relationships involving love, intimacy and sexuality. Everyone wants to be*long*, and everyone wants to be *loved*. The universal nature of the topic of *relationships*, then, will serve as an ideal framework for an open, thought-provoking evaluation.

To be sure, moving beyond superficial, theoretical ideas in order to become more transparent with ourselves will intrude on our comfort zones... and delving into the themes associated with *relationships* may do just that. We don't often talk candidly about such things, and, depending on our personal histories, discussing them could stir up painful thoughts and feelings about ourselves and others. If it does, that's okay, because we need to be able to see inside ourselves, and allow the Father to use that exposure for our eventual healing and maturity. But while a discussion about *relationships* may lead to this experience, our purpose here is not to pass judgment for past failures (which we've all had), make social commentary on controversial issues (though there is a time and place for that), or conduct an exhaustive analysis of the examples themselves. Rather, we are simply using a relevant topic to establish a common frame of reference, in order to illustrate in real-life, practical terms how we often fall short of bearing the standard of Scripture.

The following discussion will be divided into three sections corresponding to the hostile influences we have already encountered: *tradition, expediency, and rationalism.* Within each section, we'll focus on one or two specific examples that relate to the general topic of *relationships*. Aided by the use of relevant statistics and quotations, this will allow us to demonstrate and examine the effects of hostile influences, and to recognize how they often lead us to compromise God's Word in our relationships. Throughout each section, we will see how upholding the Scriptures as the standard for our relationships enables us to overcome those influences, leading us to a righteous and profoundly different destination. By the end of the examination, you will hopefully begin to perceive the extent of your own susceptibility to these hostile influences—not just in your relationships, but throughout the various areas of your life. **This is the whole point of the discussion: to raise our overall awareness of our weaknesses, and to lift up Scripture as the sole standard for effectively following Yeshua.**

THE
INFLUENCE OF
TRADITION

LET'S BEGIN OUR EVALUATION by examining the influence of *tradition* on our ability to bear the standard of Scripture. Remember that tradition—the handing down of religious, family or cultural beliefs and customs—is morally neutral in and of itself. Yet tradition has the tendency to assert itself as a voice of authority, positioning itself as a companion to or replacement for the Scriptures. Tradition advises us to sidestep God's Word and exploit Scriptural loopholes in order to maintain the illusion of obedience to God. When necessary, the traditionalist will usurp or pose as Divine authority in order to set aside the portions of Scripture that threaten his influence. It is therefore *tradition's inability to offer dependable guidance* that Mackintosh identifies as hostile toward God's Word.

The example from *relationships* that we'll use to illustrate the effects of tradition's influence is arguably the most traditional of all relationships: *marriage*. The institution of marriage is seen by many as originating from creation itself—ordained by the Creator as the foundational relationship for family, society, and the perpetuation of humanity.

> And יהוה אֱלֹהִים, *ADONAI 'Elohiym* (the LORD God) said, "[It is] not good for the man to be alone. I will make a helper for him—as his counterpart."
> ...And יהוה אֱלֹהִים, *ADONAI 'Elohiym*... took one of [the man's] ribs... [and] built up the rib... into a woman... and brought her in to the man. And the man said, "This *is* the *proper* step! bone of my bone, and flesh of my flesh!" ...Therefore a man will leave his father and his mother, and stick close to his wife, and they will become one flesh.
> בְּרֵאשִׁית GENESIS 2:18-24

The man, being alone, was incomplete, so God handcrafted the woman to be a helper and a counterpart for him. For such an exquisite creature, a man would loosen himself from his parents and reattach himself to his wife. Through the covenant-making bond of intimate relations, "they are no longer two, but one flesh." So the original marriage, as we call it, was the *permanent union* of a man to a woman, which "God joined together" (Matthew 19:6).

WHEN TRADITION FAILS

But has the traditional institution of marriage maintained this standard? Though many still claim this as marriage's historical and spiritual foundation, people no longer presume that a marriage will last. Indeed, it is commonly believed that half of all marriages in America end in divorce. While such a statistic may not be scientific, it appears to have some validity, since a 2012 report by the National Center for Health Statistics (NCHS) indicates that the probability of a first marriage surviving at least 20 years is only about 54%.

But perhaps a more helpful and practical statistic comes from Christian researcher George Barna, who took a different approach to understanding marriage and divorce in America. In a recent survey of peoples' individual marriage experiences, Barna found that

> Among adults who have been married, the study discovered that one-third (33%) have experienced at least one divorce.

In other words, one out of every three adults who has been married for any length of time has also been divorced *at least once.* This is a shocking statistic, though to some of us, it may not come as a complete surprise. While one can hardly expect Scriptural standards to be upheld among the general population, the Barna report unfortunately has even worse news for believers in Yeshua.

> Born again Christians who are not evangelical were indistinguishable from the national average on the matter of divorce: 33% have been married and divorced.... In fact, when evangelicals [Christians with a strong commitment to the fundamentals of the faith] and non-evangelical born again Christians are combined into [a single] class of born again adults, their divorce figure is [still] statistically identical to that of non-born again adults: 32% versus 33%, respectively.

Where marriage and divorce are concerned, there is no statistical difference between believers in Yeshua overall and the general population in America. How can this be? It is because for most people, marriage is not bound by the standard of Scripture, but has primarily become a social and legal institution—*a tradition.* As a social institution, marriage is subject to the changing views of society. As a legal institution, society can demand that the law reflect its evolving views. Consequently, people can now legally divorce for any *or no* reason whatsoever. Indeed, even in the most religious and traditional of marriages, husbands and wives are no longer either legally *or socially* bound to keep the wedding vows they publicly proclaimed.

The Scriptural standard for marriage—which remains unchanged—is the permanent union of a man to a woman, joined together by God. But the epidemic scale and accessibility of divorce and remarriage today **marks a further *change and failure of the tradition* of institutional marriage**. It has proven *undependable as a guide* for bearing the standard of Scripture. Indeed, Barna notes that "Americans have grown comfortable with divorce as a natural part of life.... There no longer seems to be much of a stigma attached to divorce; it is now seen as an unavoidable rite of passage." So-called "no-fault" divorce is now an embedded and accepted part of our extra-Scriptural, ever-redefining marriage *tradition.*

SIDESTEPPING SCRIPTURE

Although divorce has become integrated with the tradition of institutional marriage, nobody enjoys divorce or takes it lightly. It is traumatic and overwhelming to feel imprisoned in a troublesome marriage, yet the mere idea of breaking those marital bonds can still produce feelings of profound sorrow, grief and guilt. For the believer in Yeshua who is contemplating divorce, these feelings are also compounded by the potential for purposely violating God's Word. Why, then, with such significant obstacles to overcome, do believers feel so comfortable with divorce? It is because the *tradition* of institutional marriage has *influenced* us to usurp God's authority and sidestep the Scriptures.

Consider this letter sent to Pastor Russell D. Moore, cultural commentator and Dean of the School of Theology at The Southern Baptist Theological Seminary, asking him for advice about divorce.

> *Dear Dr. Moore,*
>
> *My wife and I are at an impasse. There's been no abandonment, no sexual immorality, and no abuse. We just don't get along. We shouldn't have married. We should have known we are incompatible. I know God hates divorce but I don't have any other option. My pastor and some Christian counselors have told me that while God hates divorce, this is the lesser of two evils because God doesn't want me to be miserable. What do you think?*
>
> *Married but Miserable*

While this letter does not divulge any details about his relationship with his wife, it does make one thing perfectly clear: Mr. Miserable has been influenced by the marriage *tradition*—the perpetuated custom and belief—that says it is better to be happy than to stay married. This widely observed tradition says that when we are miserable in our marriages, "[we] don't have any other option" but to divorce. In fact, given the choice, God allegedly prefers us to be happy.

There is no doubt that Mr. Miserable and his wife deserve our compassion. Surely, they are going through one of the most intensely emotional and gut-wrenching times of their lives. And yet, what should be obvious to us is the extent to which Mr. Miserable and his advisors are willing to go in order to preserve this particular marriage tradition. By their own admission, they are *knowingly and deliberately evading* the Scriptural principle, "God hates divorce"—a paraphrase of Malachi 2:16. After all, they reason, God may *hate* divorce, but He also *allows* it, as Scripture implies. This is a perfect example of exploiting Scriptural loopholes in order to sidestep the Word of God while maintaining the illusion of obedience.

To be sure, Deuteronomy 24:1-4—the passage from the Torah ("Law") upon which the divorce decree is based—does *not* condemn divorce. In truth, it is actually quite vague about the allowable reasons for divorce;

hence, providing the traditionalist with his loophole. Does this mean, then, that the Scriptures are open to interpretation?—that, perhaps, there may be many and various grounds for a legitimate divorce? This is the very question concerning divorce that the Pharisees put to the Master Yeshua, who laid all ambiguity to rest.

CHASING AND DEFENDING SHADOWS

In Matthew 19, the Pharisees came to test Yeshua, asking Him in verse 3, "Is it permitted for a man to send away his wife [in divorce] for every cause?"

> And He, answering, said to them, "Did you not read that He who made *them* from the begin- ning, A MALE AND A FEMALE [HE] MADE THEM, and said, 'FOR THIS REASON WILL A MAN LEAVE FATHER AND MOTHER AND BE JOINED TO HIS WIFE, AND THEY WILL BE—THE TWO—FOR ONE FLESH,' so that they are no longer two, but one flesh?"
>
> מַתִּתְיָהוּ MATTHEW 19:4-6A, QUOTING בְּרֵאשִׁית GENESIS 1:27, 2:24

So the Master begins His response to the Pharisees not with speculation and opinion, but by *bearing the standard of Scripture*. Rather than arguing the details of the marriage *tradition*, He points them back to the Word of God, and upholds the marriage *standard* that has been "from the beginning." Yeshua affirms the permanence of marriage according to God's Word as the first and final authority. As to the matter of divorce, the Master then makes His ruling:

> "Whatever, therefore, God joined together, let no man separate." מַתִּתְיָהוּ Matthew 19:6b

According to the Messiah Yeshua, God Himself joins each man and woman together by virtue of their becoming "one flesh," and no one on earth has the authority to break them apart. By nature, the union is a binding, covenantal joining. Malachi 2:14 describes the woman as the man's אֵשֶׁת בְּרִיתֶךָ, *eshet b'riytekha*—his *covenant-wife*. Paul demonstrates in Romans 7:2 that only death can legitimately release a spouse from marriage (hence, the wedding vow, "'til death do us part"). As far as Yeshua is concerned, the continuing covenantal standard for marriage is the same as that which God forged at creation: the marriage standard does not include divorce— indeed, divorce is *not supposed to be* an option.

So how is it that Scripture apparently permits divorce? Again, the Pharisees posed this very question to the Master. Pressing Him further on the issue, they asked Yeshua in verse 7, "Why, then, did Moses command to give a scroll of divorce, and to send her away?" And the Master replied,

> "Moses, for your stiffness of heart, did allow you
> to send away your wives, but from the beginning,
> it has not been so. And I say to you, that whoev-
> er sends away his wife (except for sexual unfaith-
> fulness) and marries another, commits adultery."
>
> מַתִּתְיָהוּ MATTHEW 19:8-9

We must not miss the deep truth that the Master is teaching us, especially as it concerns the influence of tradition. Yeshua has already affirmed, according to the standard of Scripture, that marriage is a permanent, unbreakable union. He then tells us that when Moses brought the Torah ("Law") to Israel, he allowed for divorce, even though "from the beginning, it has not been so." In saying this, the Master is making it clear that *God is not the creator of divorce*. Rather, in His gracious patience with Israel, He simply *tolerated* it "for your stiffness of heart." But if divorce isn't God's idea, then whose is it? The answer should be obvious: *divorce is the invention of man—a tradition.*

We should take Moses' "allowance," then, not as an open invitation to reinterpret the Scriptures regarding marriage, but merely as God's limited interaction with an *already existing tradition*. In fact, the Master Yeshua brings that divine interaction to its fullest when He declares that there are no legitimate grounds for divorce, unless the marriage covenant is *already broken* through "sexual unfaithfulness." The Messiah confirms that even though the *tradition* of marriage continues to spiral and de-evolve over time, the *Scriptural standard* for marriage —established at creation—remains the same. Yeshua's answer to the Pharisees was not meant to justify or explain Moses, but to expose how the influence of tradition led to the sidestepping of God's Word.

THE PRACTICAL EFFECTS OF TRADITION

The example of marriage and divorce vividly depicts the **hostile influence of tradition** at work. "From the beginning," God created the universal *marriage standard* that is the permanent, unbreakable joining of a man to a woman—a covenantal union that no one on earth has the authority to tear apart. Yet man **usurped and undermined God's authority by redefining** marriage, and creating a *marriage tradition* that includes the man-made invention of divorce. The deceptive counsel of **that tradition now reinterprets Scripture** for us, **exploiting** the apparent vagueness of one passage in order to **sidestep** the obvious meaning of others. Under this influence, we nevertheless try to maintain an **illusion of obedience**, asserting that God would rather we were happy and divorced than married and miserable. As Scripture's interpreter, the marriage tradition leads us to believe that God not only actively *allows* divorce, but *endorses* it. The ancient and still-evolving tradition of marriage fails as a dependable guide, because it leads us into broken covenants, and far away from the standard of Scripture.

We, the Body of Messiah, are largely persuaded to believe the tradition of marriage over God's standard, as evidenced by our participation in it. In fact, not only did Barna find that born-again Christians divorce at the same epidemic rate as the general population, but about two-thirds of all Christians also believe it is *not sinful to divorce* even if adultery has *not* been committed. This means that it is not simply those in troubled marriages who are susceptible to the tradition, but *all* who close their ears to the Master's clear and authoritative teaching. We therefore permit Scripture to be undermined, evaded, reinterpreted and sidestepped by tradition every time we ourselves entertain thoughts of divorce, or allow others' talk of divorce to go unanswered and unchallenged with the Word of God. As long as we continue to engage in marriage without the conviction that divorce is not an option, we fully testify against ourselves that we are under the influence of tradition.

What we ultimately need to realize here is that we demonstrate our susceptibility to tradition's influence not just with regard to marriage and divorce, but every time we confuse *any* social, legal, or *even religious* practice or institution with something instituted by Scripture. Just because a belief or value seems agreeable to us, and has the approval of history or society, does not mean that it originated with *or is endorsed by* God. Rather, it is a tradition's esteemed reputation and popularity with others that gives us a false sense of security in its ability to lead us toward a Scriptural life. Think about it:

▶ Have you ever felt that you "[didn't] have any other option" but to accept conventional wisdom, rather than the counsel of Scripture?

▶ Have you ever given yourself permission to follow the socially acceptable path instead of God's Word because you sincerely believed that He just wants you to be happy?

▶ Have you ever devoted yourself to a religious institution or tradition that has little or no basis in Scripture? (You might not even realize it!)

Then you, too, have fallen under the influence of tradition… an unreliable guide has steered you clear of bearing the standard of Scripture.

THE INFLUENCE OF EXPEDIENCY

WHERE *TRADITION* ENCOURAGES US to sidestep the Word of God, *expediency* persuades us to take a shortcut right through it. Remember that Mackintosh defines expediency as "the very attractive plea of doing all the good we can, without due attention to the way in which that good is done." In other words, we are being *expedient* when we do "good" according to one part of the Scriptures, but have to shortcut other parts of Scripture to do it. We justify such behavior because of the ends we gain: the tangible results and substantial proofs that God-sanctioned good is supposedly being done. But expediency influences us to reap those good fields by forsaking the allegedly fruitless path of obedience. We compromise and ignore the Word of God that we find most troubling, so that we may accomplish and celebrate the Word that we find most gratifying. Expediency undermines the Scriptures because it persuades us to do what we *think* pleases God at the expense of what the Scriptures tell us He wants. We convince ourselves that the good we are doing is all for God, when in reality, our passions and doubts pervert the desire to please God into justification for pleasing ourselves.

Moving on from an examination of the relationship of marriage, we'll now consider so-called *premarital relationships* to illustrate the effects of *expediency*. Since everyone—either now or at one time—has been "premarried," we should all be able to relate to the challenges and temptations associated with being "*single*." Sadly, the difficulties connected with singlehood are even more pronounced today, since people are delaying marriage considerably longer than in previous generations. Add to that the personal and societal pressures to marry (according to Barna, 94% of everyone over 50 has been married, as well as 73% of those over 18), and singlehood easily becomes a burden which many are anxious to unload.

For the conscientious believer in Yeshua, there is the additional matter of obedience to God, and the teachings of Scripture that apply to being single. Especially in our individualistic, hypersexualized society, choosing purity and obedience can indeed seem considerably demanding. It is wearisome to look out upon the golden fields of possible mates, knowing that God's standard for a spouse eliminates so many of them from consideration. For a time, we stand courageously and resolutely upon the "fruitless" path of obedience. Yet, as the feelings of loneliness, inadequacy and sexual frustration make it increasingly difficult to wait on God, *expediency* exploits the breach, and we soon find ourselves trying to help God move things along.

We'll begin with what may seem like a comparatively tame topic, but we'll soon see how *expediency* leads us to rapidly degrading standards.

DOING ALL THE GOOD WE CAN

Straight from the pages of Scripture, the mantras of Yeshua-believing singles are well known:

> And יהוה אֱלֹהִים, *ADONAI 'Elohiym* (the LORD God) said, "[It is] not good for the man to be alone...."
> בְּרֵאשִׁית GENESIS 2:18

and also...

> *One who* has found a wife has found [something] good, and brings out favor from ADONAI (the LORD). מִשְׁלֵי PROVERBS 18:22

So according to the Scriptures, it is natural, desirable, and *good* to be married. Indeed, it is *not* good to be alone. God *wants* us to unite forever as *one* flesh with *one* person—someone with whom we can bring forth children, walk through life, and share our entire selves... a relationship in which a man can care for his woman, and a woman can be a help to her man. Perfectly designed by God, the Father's ancient creation of marriage was meant to be fully enjoyed by His children. By definition, being married is "[something] good"—we find favor with our God when we gain the blessing of covenantal, complementary companionship.

Knowing this fundamental truth of nature and humanity, it is no wonder that singlehood evokes such anxiety. In generations past, young men and women could significantly rely upon parental influence, community support and courtship rituals to assist them in the process of finding a mate. But in today's western culture, pre-marrieds are compelled to navigate the uncertain waters of singlehood essentially on their own, primarily through the unpredictable practice of *dating*. But dating—a debate on its merits notwithstanding—does not always produce the results we desire, nor the godly spouse we seek. *Expediency*, then, seizing upon our anxiety and desperation, presents the unmarried believer in Yeshua with a clever and unique opportunity to do "[something] good" for God.

Kris Swiatocho, director of The Singles Network Ministries, confesses that she used to engage regularly in the practice commonly known as *missionary dating*. A relatively benign practice along the spectrum of premarital relationships, missionary dating is a form of opposite-gender evangelism, in which dating is used as a pretext to share Yeshua—"[something] good" for God. But Swiatocho, like most believers who intentionally or inadvertently practice missionary dating, was *in reality* using the pretext of evangelism as an *excuse* to date unbelievers. Recounting how she formerly justified this spin, she explains,

> I seemed to be on a mission to get guys "saved," "walking with God" and "growing in their faith." So what is wrong with that? I mean, we are supposed to witness and help lead others to Christ, right? *So everywhere we go, we tell everyone about Christ. We warn them and teach them with all the wisdom God has given us, for we want to present them to God, perfect in their relationship to Christ. Colossians 1:28 [NLT]*

So, at least on the surface, Swiatocho saw dating un-believers (or "name-only" believers) as a mission field—her opportunity to take advantage of being single, and do "all the good" for God she could do.

Who can argue with the logic? No one can capture the attention of a single man like a single woman (and vice versa), making pre-marrieds uniquely qualified to "evangelize" one another. And since Genesis 2:18 says it's "not good" to be alone, and Colossians 1:28 says it's good to "tell everyone" about Messiah, then, as the thinking goes, a believer dating an unbeliever is actual-ly "[something] good." Every date, then, becomes "sub-stantial proof" that the kingdom of God is advancing—"tangible results" that God is being served. Perhaps the harvest of love and marriage is not being reaped, but abandoning the fruitless path of obedience is worth it if it means people are getting saved!

THE PATH OF OBEDIENCE

The reality, however, is that this approach to relation-ships—despite the true motives of the heart—hardly ever produces salvations (and if it does, can even those good ends really justify the means?) Rather, an honest evaluation reveals that this method consistently pro-duces a *fruitless* string of self-deceptions, romantic failures, lowered standards, and compromised convictions. As Swiatocho concedes,

> I guess I have always known in my heart that any guy who didn't love God, didn't put Christ first and wasn't growing in his relationship with Christ by the evidence of his fruit is someone I shouldn't date. However, I did anyway. [...I would tell myself,] "At least he isn't [a] bad person..." [and,] "I know if I can just be the example, he will change." [W]hen was I going to figure it out? How many guys would I date in the hopes of either getting them "saved" or "walking right" with God? How long was it going to take for me to listen to God?

The problem with trying to justify these kinds of premarital relationships—by way of Genesis 2, or Colossians 1, or any other "good" thing—is that we have to be *expedient* to do it... and take a shortcut right past 2 Corinthians 6:14-15:

> [Do] not become unequally yoked with unbelievers. For what partnership *is there* between righteousness and wickedness? and what does light share with darkness? and what agreement has Messiah with Belial? or what part does a believer [have in common] with an unbeliever?

Though Paul is not explicitly addressing *premarital* relationships here, the application should be obvious.

Entering into a romantic or premarital relationship with someone constitutes an emotional, spiritual—and, too often, physical—bond. And when that bond forms between a believer and an unbeliever (or a "name-only" believer), it blatantly violates the standard of Scripture. Paul also advises us in 1Corinthians 15:33, "Be not led astray: 'Evil associations corrupt good character.'" An unequal yoking is more likely to have a deleterious effect on the believer than to result in the salvation of a love interest. The truth is, despite any situational or superficial common interests, and regardless of any supposedly pure motives we may have, believers and unbelievers ultimately have *nothing* in common. Therefore, any intimate partnership between two such people is wholly unequal... precariously straddling a vast and unbridgeable abyss.

Pursuing premarital relationships with unbelievers, then, is a result of the influence of *expediency*. While the path of obedience clearly says to not become unequally yoked with unbelievers, expediency offers an opportune shortcut by which to justify such associations. Worn down by desperation and the unmet goals of singlehood, we give in and allow *expediency* to begin coloring the way we perceive and apply the Scriptures about marriage. Since being alone is "not good" (Genesis 2) and it is "good" to find a spouse (Proverbs 18), we bend these to mean that God wants us to do "all the good we can" in seeking a significant other. Like King Saul and his sacrifices of disobedience, the prospect of bringing an unbeliever to Messiah invites us to obscure our self-seeking motives behind the goal of doing "[something] good." In the end, *expediency* leads us to believe that it's better to do something we presume God wants, than to obey Him by doing nothing. Expediency pleads with us to generate tangible results at any cost—even if it means we have to relax Scripture's requirements, compromise our convictions, and lower the Standard a bit to do it.

WHEN SHORTCUTS BECOME SIDETRACKS

Unfortunately, even the briefest of shortcuts can take a turn for the worse. Expediency often influences us in a direction that has nothing to do with doing good for God, but only with pleasing ourselves. In the case of premarital relationships, the consuming desire for emotional, mental and physical intimacy can mislead us into justifying all kinds of behavior that we know are contrary to the Word of God.

While the boundaries of dating may appear somewhat blurry at times, there is nothing at all nebulous about the lines we cross with *premarital sex*. And yet, a *staggering* number of unmarried *believers* today are habitually having sexual relations without marriage. In his *Relevant* magazine article "(Almost) Everyone's

Doing It," Tyler Charles casts a sobering light on the astonishing and bewildering statistics.

> [A] recent study reveals that 88 percent of [all] unmarried young adults (ages 18-29) are having sex. The same study, conducted by The National Campaign to Prevent Teen and Unplanned Pregnancy, reveals the number doesn't drop much among Christians. Of those surveyed who self-identify as "evangelical," 80 percent say they have had sex. *Eighty percent.* ...even though, according to a recent Gallup poll, 76 percent of evangelicals believe sex outside of marriage is morally wrong.

Eight in every ten young adult believers have engaged in premarital sex! It is almost beyond belief. Not only should we find this statistic alarming in and of itself, but once again, it demonstrates how we as the Body of Messiah have failed to significantly distinguish ourselves from the world.

And as if all that weren't shocking enough, consider this bit of number crunching: if only 76 percent of believers think that premarital sex is wrong (which means that the inverse, 24 percent, are okay with it), this means that at least 56 percent of the believers who have engaged in premarital sex (80 percent minus 24 percent) are also flat-out *hypocrites*. **In other words, more than**

half of all young adult believers think that premarital sex is wrong, *but do it anyway*. How can this be?

To make matters worse, Charles goes on to point out that of those believers who have had premarital sex, "64 percent have done so within the last year and 42 percent are in a current sexual relationship." Not only are such believers promiscuous *and* hypocritical, but they intentionally remain in premarital relationships that perpetuate sexual immorality. How do believers in Messiah justify habitual participation in something they know to be wrong? It's easy... when we're under the influence of *expediency*.

It begins the same way: as we walk the path of purity—flanked by opportunity's ripe and golden fields—those feelings of loneliness, inadequacy and sexual frustration make the road of obedience seem substantially barren... and absent of God. Then, like the serpent in the Garden, *expediency* helps us to twist the Word of God in our minds: Genesis 2:18 now whispers that it's "not good" to *feel lonely*; Proverbs 18:22 suddenly suggests that *physical intimacy* would absolutely be "[something] good." Taking that first step from the path, we are hesitant and unsure of venturing too far. But soon, the urge to justify our deviation fades, and we are overcome by a flood of sensual and emotional affirmation. The heavenly experience of becoming *one flesh* assures us it is all "good"... *welcome to expediency!*

We need to realize that premarital sex isn't just about sex, it's a *shortcut of expediency* to "one flesh"... *marriage:* the *permanent union* of a man to a woman, joined together by God. This is where the vast majority of unmarrieds innately want to go, and our physical cravings—along with the emotional, mental, and spiritual desire for intimacy—powerfully drive us there. That drive is normal, natural, and *good*, but God did not intend for it to culminate in anything but *permanent* union. We can try to convince ourselves that a monogamous sexual relationship without marriage isn't immoral; or that it's acceptable to have premarital sex when it's with the person we're expecting to marry. But what will such a marriage be built upon if it was conceived in the bed of *compromise?* Or how many monogamous sexual relationships can we have before it becomes *adulterous?* No matter how we try to justify it, we can't escape the standard of Scripture, which says that the act of becoming "one flesh" joins us together *permanently* in the eyes of God. This is why Paul—referencing God's standard for marriage established at creation—pointedly asks us,

> Have you not known that your bodies are members of Messiah? Having taken, then, the members of the Messiah, should I make *them* members of a prostitute? Let it not be! Have you not known that he who is joined to the prostitute is one body

[with her]? "For they will be," He says, "the two for
one flesh." 1CORINTHIANS 6:15-16, QUOTING GENESIS 2:24

Marriage, in God's eyes, is not a ceremonial or legal
transaction—it is the consummation of the marriage
act... becoming "one flesh" (cf. Exodus 22:16). If we
become "one body" with a prostitute by uniting our
members with her, how much more do we become "one
flesh"—that is, *married*—through sexual relations with
the one we claim to love? Then, when that monogamous
relationship is succeeded by another, or our wedding
plans change because we (or our betrothed) end up mar-
rying somebody else, we have willfully *separated what
God has joined together* (Matthew 19:6), and our shortcut has delivered us to adultery's doorstep (see Matthew
5:32, 19:9; Mark 10:11-12; Luke 16:18).

Though expediency attempts to transport us quickly from the fruitlessness of singlehood to the fulfillment
of marriage, we can never be certain of its route, or its
host of unintended consequences. What we *can* know
for sure, is that when we "burn [with desire]" and "cannot contain [ourselves]," the Scriptural response is not
to have sex... it's to *get married!* (see 1Corinthians 7:8-
9). Premarital sex violates God's standard because it
allows singles to experience the *act* of marriage without
recognizing and agreeing to the *covenantal union* of marriage. We lose sight of that standard, then, when we ex-

pediently try to have "all the good [benefits of marriage] we can, without due attention to the way in which that good is done." As the Scripture says,

> Marriage *is* [to be] honored by all, and the [marriage] bed undefiled; and [those who are] sexually promiscuous and adulterers, God will judge.
> עִבְרִים Hebrews 13:4

THE PRACTICAL EFFECTS OF EXPEDIENCY

The example of premarital relationships graphically illustrates the **hostile influence of expediency** at work. In the beginning, God said, "[it is] not good for the man to be alone," and established *marriage* as something that is both desirable and *good* for humankind. But when our desire for a godly spouse goes unfulfilled, *expediency* persuades us to forsake God's Word and the **lonely, fruitless path of obedience** for the golden fields of companionship... and compromise. Soon, we are doing **"all the good we can,"** convinced that our pursuit of an unbelieving or promiscuous mate is somehow (or will someday become) pleasing to God. We feel justified by the **tangible results** of the relationship—its resemblance to the "one flesh" of marriage is **substantial proof** that "[something] good" is being done. But in reality, *expediency* has raced us past the holy and unadulterated Word of God. It has influenced us to **shortcut the Scriptures** and bypass God's standard for our sexual purity and our spouse's spiritual equality. Despite any insistence to the contrary, premarital relationships of expediency do not result in doing "good" for God. Instead, they lead us further into self-delusion and self-pleasure at the expense of the standard of Scripture.

We, the Body of Messiah, are largely persuaded to pursue the expediency of premarital relationships over God's standard, as evidenced by our participation in it. Not only did The National Campaign survey reveal that a staggering 80% of young believing adults have had premarital sex, but, according to Charles, "an alarming number of unmarried Christians [30%] are getting pregnant.... But perhaps the most disturbing statistic for the Church: 65 percent of the women obtaining abortions identify themselves as either Protestant or Catholic.... That's 650,000 abortions obtained by Christians every year. The pregnancy stats are shocking to many—and the abortion stats horrifying—but the root problem is the *willingness* to have sex before marriage. Without sex, pregnancies and abortions don't happen." Sexual promiscuity, leading to adulterous relationships... Out-of-wedlock pregnancies, leading to abortions... Once we start down the path of least resistance, our accelerated pursuit of "tangible results" hurls us toward dire and immoral consequences. As long as we continue to disregard or distort the Scriptures while engaging in the world's pattern of premarital relations, we will go on offering many "substantial proofs" against ourselves.

What we fundamentally need to catch hold of here is that we demonstrate our susceptibility to expediency's influence not just with regard to premarital relationships, but every time we justify our disobedience of Scripture with the "good" we are seeking to do in its place. Just because we might be seeing what appear to be Scriptural outcomes does not mean that we haven't bypassed or shortcut Scripture in order to accomplish them. On the contrary, something that may be "good" in one context becomes completely and utterly defiled by our self-seeking motives and violation of Scripture. Consider this:

- ► Have you ever compromised Scriptural principles under the pretext of being more relatable or less offensive to unbelievers?

- ► Have you ever allowed your emotions or aspirations to affect the way you understand and act upon God's Word?

- ► Have you ever disregarded what you perceived as irrelevant Scriptural commands in order to accomplish what you concluded were greater and more substantial things for God?

Then you, too, have fallen under the influence of expediency... you tried to justify doing "[something] good," but at the expense of bearing the standard of Scripture.

THE INFLUENCE OF RATIONALISM

WHERE *EXPEDIENCY PERSUADES US* to take a shortcut right through the Word of God, and *tradition* encourages us to sidestep around it, *rationalism* convinces us to take a different road altogether, sharply veering away from the straight and level path of Scripture. Remember that Mackintosh defines rationalism as "the supremacy of man's reason"—that man's reason has no equal, and may therefore "sit in judgment upon the Word of God." Rationalism believes it has the right to ignore and subvert Scripture's authority. By challenging the supremacy of Scripture, rationalism tries to make the perfect, unbreakable wisdom of God appear foolish and unreasonable to men's minds. If rationalism appears to trust in the Word of God at all, it is only to the extent that Scripture happens to agree with its opinions. When man's reason and God's Word are in conflict, *rationalism* arrogantly brands Scripture as *defective*. What is the result? "God is shut out of His own book, if He says anything which poor, blind, perverted reason cannot reconcile with her own conclusions."

Continuing on now from our brief examinations of *marriage and divorce* and *premarital relationships*, we'll now consider the foremost social, political, and moral relationship issue of our day to illustrate the effects of *rationalism*. At the time of this writing, the global community is experiencing a surge in momentum toward the complete acceptance and normalization of *homosexuality*. Indeed, in the United States alone, Gallup reported in 2011 that for the first time, a majority of Americans (53%) believed that same-sex marriage should be legal. As of November 6, 2012, nine U.S. states plus the District of Columbia now allow same-sex marriage (ten U.S. states have approved constitutional amendments banning same-sex marriage). And it is most certainly a sign of the times that on May 9, 2012, President Barack Obama became the first sitting U.S. president to openly declare his support for legalizing same-sex marriage. The normalization of homosexuality is (at least for the time being) a polarizing issue, to be sure. But while it is usually framed as a socio-political matter, many within the Body of Messiah are now beginning to wonder if homosexuality—like divorce and premarital sex before it—is really as immoral as they've been led to believe.

Especially among Christians who have friends or relatives who identify as homosexual, it has become a deeply personal issue—so much so that a growing number of believers are now saying that God accepts homosexuality in the context of a committed, permanent, loving relationship. Such was the conviction in 2009, for example, when the Evangelical Lutheran Church of America (ELCA) and the Episcopal Church both voted to permit the ordination of *non-celibate* homosexual ministers; the Presbyterian Church (PCUSA) followed suit in 2011... and that's just in the United States. Part of this shift is a response to both the real and perceived ostracizing, unloving, and "unchristian" treatment by believers toward those who identify as homosexual. But instead of addressing the issue of how to confront a sinful lifestyle with the uncompromising love of Yeshua, the solution has been to change the way we see homosexuality, and push for the normalization *and celebration* of unscriptural behavior. What for millennia has been understood from Scripture as a wholly condemnable sexual sin is now being widely reconsidered in a new light —the dazzling and brilliant light of man's reason; the mesmerizing glow of *rationalism*.

A WAY THAT SEEMS RIGHT

Regrettably, what the Scriptures plainly present, and what believers are starting to "see" are two entirely different things. Despite ongoing efforts to recontextualize and reinterpret Scripture's position, the unmistakable fact is that God's Word clearly and explicitly condemns the practice of homosexual acts. As Moses states in the strongest possible terms,

> And a man who lies [down] with a male as one lies [down] with a woman; both of them have done [a] disgusting thing; they are certainly [to be] put to death; their blood *is* on them.
> וַיִּקְרָא LEVITICUS 20:13 (CF. 18:22)

The straightforward instruction of Scripture is unavoidable and unanimous: homosexual acts are condemnable in the eyes of God. Indeed, as if Moses' teaching were somehow insufficient, consider Paul, who patently labels homosexual relationships in 1Timothy 1:8-11 as "contrary to sound teaching." And again, in 1Corinthians 6:9-11, Paul unequivocally denounces such acts as an unrighteousness that excludes one from "inherit[ing] the Reign of God." The Good News is that through the Master Yeshua, there is hope for change, cleansing and reconciliation with God for those participating in homosexuality (see 1Corinthians 6:11). The "bad news" is that everything Scripture says about homosexual relationships is consistent: they are unnatural, unrighteous, sinful and disgusting. To some, such a characterization may seem intensely hateful, intolerant and offensive, but the unambiguous fact remains that the *objective* Word of God—as archived for us in the Scriptures—says that homosexual behavior is wrong.

And yet, despite such forthrightness and clarity, even Christian leaders are increasingly questioning the plain teaching of Scripture. Take, for example, Pastor Chuck Smith, Jr., son of the Calvary Chapel movement's founder, Chuck Smith. When asked in 2005, "Are there gay Christians?" he replied,

> The easy answer is, "Yes, and there are Christians who have committed adultery, there are Christians who have stolen." But that's the easy answer, because that implies that homosexuality is morally wrong. My answer is, I'm still looking at it. On the one hand, I'm up against biblical passages [condemning homosexuality] that I need to investigate more thoroughly. On the other hand, I know many practicing homosexuals. I know two

> young men who've been monogamous partners
> for seven years. They've adopted a son who is
> thriving. They're good dads, they're good people,
> they have asked Jesus into their hearts and seek to
> live Christian lives.

Though Smith found himself "up against biblical passages," he was nevertheless unable to consider homosexual relationships in the same vein as adultery or stealing—that is, as something that is "morally wrong." Why? Because his personal experience with those he knew as "practicing homosexuals" seemed to be at odds with the Word of God. Indeed, how could believers who are "good dads," "good people," and "monogamous partners" not be acceptable to Jesus just because they commit homosexual acts? The answer is: because Scripture says they're not... and it is the influence of *rationalism* which leads us to believe otherwise. Pastor Smith was "still looking at" the issue and not accepting God's Word because he took the Scriptures "on the one hand," and his feelings, experience, and personal sense of right and wrong "on the other." He elevated his own reasoning and perception of reality first to make it *equal* with Scripture, and then *rationalism* tipped the scale, overtaking the Word of God as the authoritative standard. Indeed, within five years of making these remarks, Smith began publically standing as a "straight ally" for *non-celibate* homosexual Christians.

But where Smith was moved to suppress Scripture according to personal experience, Brian McLaren thought it wise to discount the Word in view of man's enlightened reason. McLaren, a leading figure in the emerging church movement and recognized by Time Magazine as one of the 25 Most Influential Evangelicals in America, was formerly confused about the legitimacy of homosexual relationships. Before eventually coming down on the side of same-sex marriage and non-celibate homosexual Christians, he confessed,

> Frankly, many of us [emerging church leaders] don't know what we should think about homosexuality. We've heard all sides but no position has yet won our confidence so that we can say "it seems good to the Holy Spirit and us." [If] we think that there may actually be a legitimate context for some homosexual relationships, we know that the biblical arguments are nuanced and multilayered… we aren't sure if or where lines are to be drawn…. Perhaps we need a five-year moratorium on making pronouncements…. We'll keep our ears attuned to scholars in biblical studies, theology, ethics, psychology, genetics, sociology, and related fields….

Why was McLaren unable to know what to think? Because his search for answers began not with *Scripture*, but with a *rationalized presumption:* "there may actually

be a legitimate context for some homosexual relationships." Amid the noise of this preconceived idea, the
plain teaching of Scripture became indecipherable ("we
aren't sure if or where lines are to be drawn")—the clear
message of God's Word, undefined ("the biblical argu-
ments are nuanced and multilayered"). "No position"—
not even the "side" of Scripture—could win his confidence because the clamoring sounds of *rationalism* were
drowning out the lone voice of God. What was McLar-
en's solution to the discord? Pump up the volume! Deaf-
en wisdom's ears with the ceaseless speculations of
"scholars in biblical studies, theology, ethics, psycholo-
gy, genetics, sociology, and related fields." Surely, there
must be more to God's Word than the self-evident sense
of the text! Obviously, God's true will can be discerned
by mining the unfathomable riches of man's reason! For
McLaren, considering the plain meaning of Scripture
seemed not to be an option. When Scripture failed to
provide the answer to his supposition, *rationalism* sug-
gested he entertain other voices.

But the true will of God is *not* hidden or obscured,
and no amount of scrutiny or experimentation will cause
it to change. Indeed,

> ...from the creation of the world, the invisible
> things of Him—being understood by [way of]
> the [visible] things [that have been] made—
> are plainly seen... to [the point of men's lack of

> knowledge] being inexcusable. Because [despite]
> having known God, they did not glorify *Him* as
> God, nor gave [Him] thanks, but were [instead]
> made empty in their reasonings, and their un-
> comprehending heart was darkened. Claiming to
> be wise, they were made fools. ROMANS 1:20-22

If even the "invisible things" of God "are plainly seen," how much more are "the [visible] things [that
have been] made"? So obvious is the distortion and re-
pudiation of nature in homosexuality that men are completely without excuse. In our rebellious denial of the
"plainly seen," our "reasonings" are "made empty;" our
"uncomprehending heart... darkened." Then *rationalism* leads us astray, causing us to proclaim ourselves as
"wise." And yet, by failing to acknowledge the creation
of God, we make ourselves utter fools. To this—the arrogant assertion of man's supreme reason—God has His
response. Paul continues,

> Therefore God also gave them up, in the desires
> of their hearts, to uncleanness, to degrade their
> bodies among themselves: [those] who changed
> the truth of God into a falsehood, and honored
> and served the created-thing rather than the Cre-
> ator.... Because of this, God gave them up to de-
> grading affections, for even their females changed
> the natural use into that [which is] against nature;
> and likewise the males also (having left the natu-

ral use of the female) burned in the longing toward one another—males with males working
shame[less acts]—and in themselves receiving the
reward of their error that was fit [for their per-
version]. And, as they did not approve of having
God in [their] knowledge, God gave them up to
a failed mind, to do what ought not to be done....
ROMANS 1:24-28

BRANDING SCRIPTURE AS "DEFECTIVE"

It is this very same "failed mind" which brashly
stands nose to nose with the Word of God, and, spewing
contempt in its face, declares, "You are defective." Such
is the pronouncement by William M. Kent, as published
in the *Report of the Committee to Study Homosexuality to
the General Council on Ministries of the United Methodist
Church*, dated August 24, 1991. Over twenty years ago,
Kent contended that

...the scriptural texts in the Old and New Testa-
ments condemning homosexual practice are neither inspired by God nor otherwise of enduring
Christian value. Considered in the light of the
best biblical, theological, scientific, and social
knowledge, the biblical condemnation of homosexual practice is better understood as represent-
ing time and place bound cultural prejudice.

In one swift stroke, Kent attempts to slit Scripture's throat, then carve it up into little, non-authoritative pieces. With the steely blade of *rationalism*, he stabs at the texts condemning homosexual practice, saying that not only do they have no *value* for believers today, but that *they do not even constitute the Word of God*. In Kent's view, the specific passages in question cannot have been "inspired by God" for one simple reason: we have *better knowledge* available to us, and that knowledge is opposed to the Scriptures. "The biblical condemnation of homosexual practice is better understood," Kent says, when we consider it "in the light of the best biblical, theological, scientific, and social *knowledge*." Does Kent admit that Scripture condemns homosexual relationships? He absolutely does. *He just doesn't believe that those particular passages of Scripture were inspired by God.* Yes, rationalism insists that we can discern the difference between those segments of Scripture that are inspired by God and those that aren't because we have "the best... knowledge" of man! Those inconvenient passages of Scripture with which we disagree *must be* uninspired and irrelevant, because *we know better.*

Thus, *rationalism brands Scripture as defective*, granting us our own authority to disregard *and redefine* God's Word in light of man's superior reasoning. The slippery slope here should be obvious: once rationalism causes us to doubt the authenticity of one verse of Scripture, how can our supreme minds confidently affirm the credibility of the next? It's one thing to scrutinize an ancient, foreign-language manuscript for textual and linguistic accuracy, but to disparage its *content* just because it deviates from our "enlightened" sensibilities is an outright denial of its power and authority. Ultimately, such "clobber passages" will not simply be tolerated as insignificant, or relegated to another culture and time. Eventually, we will seek to *crucify* them in order to assert our superiority over God.

This is exactly what Gary David Comstock promotes in his defense of non-celibate homosexual Christians and so-called "Gay Theology." A self-identifying homosexual, as well as a Professor of Sociology and United Church of Christ chaplain at Wesleyan University, Comstock writes,

> Not to recognize, critique, and condemn Paul's equation of godlessness with homosexuality is dangerous. To remain within our respective Christian traditions and not challenge those passages that degrade and destroy us [homosexuals] is to contribute to our own oppression.... These passages will be brought up and used against us again and again until Christians demand their removal from the biblical canon, or, at the very least, formally discredit their authority to prescribe behavior.

Comstock does not deny that Paul "[equates] god-lessness with homosexuality." On the contrary, he encourages Christians to "recognize" it, and rightly so. But his acknowledgement rapidly escalates past a baseless "critique" of Scripture into its audacious "challenge"— one expressly designed to bring about Scripture's permanent "condemnation."

In Comstock's view, Scripture is "dangerous." For him and other self-identifying Christian homosexuals, certain passages of Scripture are *degrading, oppressive* and *destructive*. Comstock's final solution? Kill or be killed—take those "dangerous" Scriptures that "degrade," and "destroy," and "demand their removal from the biblical canon, or, at the very least, formally discredit their authority to prescribe behavior." Unlike Kent, Comstock isn't explicitly questioning the inspiration of Scripture… no, he just wants to rip the "dangerous" parts out of The Book and hang them on a tree! And if for some reason, people aren't willing to take things quite that far, we should at least strip the Word naked, whip it to a bloody pulp, then parade it through the streets in utter humiliation. Comstock's failure to bear the standard of Scripture is painfully obvious: he alleges the defective inferiority of God's Word, *rationalizing* that if Scripture condemns his sinful actions, then Scripture is in error, and therefore fit for its own condemnation.

But what Comstock refuses to accept is the essential truth as encapsulated by Wheaton College Provost Stanton Jones: "[W]hen there is a gap between the biblical teaching and our behavior, it is we (and not the Bible) who are wrong and in need of correction." Indeed! Scripture is *never* subject to the rationalizations of men. Rather, it is wholly within Scripture's jurisdiction as the only rightful "authority to prescribe behavior" to be a voice of destruction for sin. What Comstock calls "dangerous" and "oppress[ive]" is not some random or prejudicial set of man-made regulations. He is instead calling for the execution or disgracing of the absolute standard of God— He is sitting in judgment on the authority of Scripture.

DENYING THE AUTHORITY OF SCRIPTURE

This is where it all leads: in order for the influence of *rationalism* to overpower our hearts and seduce our minds, we have to deny the only thing standing in its way... the sole and final authority of Scripture. Before we can switch allegiances and place ourselves under our own contrived authority—one which we ourselves control—we have no choice but to reject and disparage the perfect Word of God. This is exactly what Luke Timothy Johnson had to do in order to rationalize his own daughter's decision "to claim her sexual identity as a lesbian." Johnson, the R.W. Woodruff Professor of

New Testament and Christian Origins at the Candler School of Theology at Emory University, takes rationalism to nearly incomprehensible heights to make room for a hopeless father's acceptance of his beloved daughter's sin.

> I think it important to state clearly that we do, in fact, reject the straightforward commands of Scripture, and appeal instead to another authority when we declare that same-sex unions can be holy and good. And what exactly is that authority? We appeal explicitly to the weight of our own experience and the experience thousands of others have witnessed to, which tells us that to claim our own sexual orientation is in fact to accept the way in which God has created us. By so doing, we explicitly reject as well the premises of the scriptural statements condemning homosexuality— namely, that it is a vice freely chosen, a symptom of human corruption, and disobedience to God's created order.

In an examination of how the hostile influence of rationalism challenges our submission to Scripture, there may be no clearer example than this. Johnson unabashedly and unapologetically states that he does "in fact, reject the straightforward commands of Scripture." That is, he denies the authority of Scripture, which plainly instructs us concerning the sinfulness of homosexual relationships. By Johnson's own admission, Scripture is absolutely clear in its condemnation of homosexuality as a behavior of *choice*, marked by moral *corruption* and blatant *disobedience* of God. On this point, Johnson simply acknowledges what Scripture plainly says, then discards it, offering no challenge, no excuse, and no defense.

So how does he get around it? How can he claim that God intentionally creates some people with "sexual orientation[s]" that directly violate "God's created order"? He "appeal[s] instead to another authority." He says to Scripture, *I do not recognize your authority because you deny what I know to be true*, and instead turns to "another authority" that supports his own reasoning—one that says long-lasting, caring, fruitful homosexual relationships are not only acceptable to God, but "holy and good."

"And what exactly is that authority?" Johnson asks. What authority is so supreme—so much greater than Scripture—that it has the sovereignty to override Scripture's "straightforward commands" whenever they contradict our beliefs? **"We appeal explicitly to the weight of our own experience and the experience thousands of others have witnessed to." Yes, Johnson says that the authority of "our own experience" outweighs the authority of Scripture**—that there are limitations and *boundaries* to Scripture's jurisdiction. And what's more, he yields to this so-called authority knowing full well that "by so doing, we explicitly reject as well the premises of the scriptural statements condemning homosexuality." This is not an example of Scriptural ignorance, or one that attempts to reinterpret the plain meaning of the texts. No, Johnson simply extracts those statements from the pages of Scripture, calmly sets them on fire with a lighted match, and then drops the flaming excerpts in the closest wastebin, leaving them to smolder and slowly snuff out of existence. Once again, the imbalanced scales of rationalism favor *the reasoning of personal experience* over the supreme and sufficient standard of Scripture.

And yet, Johnson isn't anywhere near finished. What is most flabbergasting about his astonishing position is not the fact that he rejects Scripture in order to submit to "experience," but the *rationalization* he uses to justify it. How can Johnson so casually dismiss Scriptural authority? Because in some kind of theological schizophrenia, he sees *obedience to God* and *obedience to Scripture* as two entirely separate things.

> We are fully aware of the weight of scriptural evidence pointing away from our position, yet place our trust in the power of the living God to reveal as powerfully through personal experience and testimony as through written texts. [If] the letter of Scripture cannot find room for the activity

of the living God in the transformation of human lives, then trust and obedience must be paid to the living God rather than to the words of Scripture.

Just what, exactly, is Johnson saying here? First, he asserts that God can (and does) reveal His will for us "as powerfully through personal experience" as through Scripture—even (and especially) when "the weight of scriptural evidence" contradicts our experience. In other words, whatever we think, or observe, or encounter, or undergo is now a legitimate conduit for *direct revelation* from God. The Creator reveals his *objective* will through *subjective* personal experience—experience that differs from person to person. In Johnson's view, personal experience goes far beyond having the ability to *confirm* Scriptural truth. As long as our experience affirms what we *believe* to be authoritative, divine revelation, then that's exactly what it is. Should we, then, weigh such "revelation" against Scripture? Johnson's fine with that. But if our "experience" turns out be in conflict with The Book—no problem!—God can "reveal [His will] as powerfully through personal experience and testimony as through written texts." Such is the confounding conviction of *rationalism!* No doubt, the Spirit can (and does) reveal truth to our hearts and minds to which we had previously been blind, but that act is a far cry from being given *experiential revelation* from God *that is contrary to His very own Word.*

Second, Johnson makes the most bizarre declaration of all: If Scripture "cannot find room for the activity of… God," then we need to trust and obey "God rather than… Scripture." Hear again this bewildering proposition: we need to trust and obey God, *rather than* Scripture. Johnson is juxtaposing "the activity of the living God" with "the words of Scripture," as if it were somehow possible for a righteous, trustworthy God to *act* in a way that *contradicts* His own Word… as if Scripture is too rigid ("cannot find room") to accommodate its Author. How do you separate God from His Word, much less cause Him to stand opposed to His own message? According to Johnson, you can. Under the reign of man's supreme reason, obedience to God and obedience to Scripture are—stupefyingly—two different things. And the worst part? Sometimes, in order to truly obey God, you have to *disobey* ("explicitly reject") Scripture's authority, and submit instead to *personal experience.*

What we desperately need to apprehend here is that Johnson, in his doctrinal dementia, is merely admitting to what most of us do stealthily every day, as we deny the authority of Scripture. When we can't "find room" in the written Word for the things we want to do, how often do we appeal to "another authority"—either by ignoring the Word, justifying our behavior, or invoking the special pleading of "personal experience"? Indeed, many of us will praise the Scriptures with our lips, swearing our allegiance to them, and then deny them the next moment with our defiant actions. This demonstrates exactly what Johnson articulates: that we are willing to obey Scripture only as long as it weighs less than our own will. The moment our knowledge, *reasoning* and "personal experience" exceed the weight of Scripture's authority, we *rationalize* all manner of delirium to circumvent it. We may not be as overtly calculated and deliberate in our defiance as Johnson, but the net result is the same: we trust and obey our own thoughts, opinions and experiences, rather than the words of Scripture—we assert the supremacy of man's reason over the authority of God's Word.

THE PRACTICAL EFFECTS OF RATIONALISM

The example of homosexual relationships vividly depicts the **hostile influence of rationalism** at work. Scripture plainly teaches that homosexual behavior is morally wrong and condemnable in the eyes of God. But when we presume—in spite of that straightforward instruction—that there may still be a legitimate context for homosexual relationships, we elevate our own thinking above Scripture, thereby declaring that **man's reason has no equal**. If God's Word disagrees with our "better knowledge," or conflicts with what we "know" to be true, we *rationalize* that **Scripture must be defective**— that God couldn't possibly have inspired the Scriptural passages condemning homosexual relationships. As we arrogantly **sit in judgment of Scripture**—disregarding it, redefining it, even declaring it "dangerous" and "destructive"—we **deny that Scripture has sole authority** to determine morality and "prescribe behavior" for our lives; we **impose boundaries** on the breadth of Scripture's knowledge and jurisdiction. Under the hallucinatory influence of *rationalism*, we believe it is reasonable to disobey God's written Word in order to obey His alleged will. So we appeal to the subjective "revelation" of *personal experience*, even when it blatantly—and self-admittedly—contradicts the objective revelation of Scripture.

Wisdom has a sober warning for those deluded by such rationalism: "There is a way in front of a man's face [that seems] right, but its eventual end *are ways* of death" (Proverbs 14:12). Where else will conceit and contempt for God's Word lead, but the grave? Indeed, the rationalism being used to justify homosexual relationships erodes the authority of Scripture to the point of utter impotence. Case in point, as Stanton Jones documents,

> Gay Episcopalian New Testament scholar L. William Countryman... concludes that "The gospel

allows no rule against... bestiality [sex with ani-
mals], polygamy, homosexual acts," or "pornography." On such matters, he argues, we are not
free to "impose our codes on others."

If Scripture can be reduced to non-authoritative
"codes" of feeble, man-made morality, then there truly
is no supreme and sufficient standard to bear. Suddenly, "all things are permitted for me" (1Corinthians 6:12),
and will soon be eligible for full acceptance and immediate *normalization*—and it will not stop with homosexuality. Once the authority of Scripture is rationalized
down to a status equal to or beneath man's reason, we
will quickly find ourselves forced to agree with the de-
praved values and viewpoints of the world. As Southern
Baptist Theological Seminary president Albert Mohler
rightly observes, "We should expect the secular world,
which is at war with God's truth, to be eager in its efforts
to rationalize lust, and to seek legitimacy and social
sanction for its sexual sins. We should be shocked, however, that many within the Church now seek to accomplish the same purpose, and to join in common cause
with those openly at war with God's truth." There is no
stopping our de-evolution into unbridled perversity as
long as worldly *rationalism* continues to influence our
thinking, and undermine our trust in the Word of God.

It is absolutely critical that we grasp the reality of
this. The rationalism that is running amok in the Body

of Messiah today—the rationalism which says that God actually calls something *right* which Scripture clearly portrays as *wrong*—is not limited to those championing homosexual relationships. The fact is, we permit Scripture to be rendered defective, considered irrelevant, and judged to be in error by rationalism every time we allow our emotions, reasonings and personal experience to tell us God approves of that which Scripture forbids. Indeed, instead of submitting to what Scripture says even when we disagree with it or find it unfair, we invite the supposedly incomparable knowledge of mankind to correct the allegedly faulty wisdom of God. Think about it:

▸ When you've been "up against biblical passages" that plainly contradict your own point of view, have you ever tried finding a more loving or tolerant explanation for them?

▸ In trying to discern the truth of a matter, have you ever weighed the Scriptures "on the one hand," and your feelings, experience, or personal sense of right and wrong "on the other"?

▸ Have you ever reinterpreted or just flat out rejected the straightforward teaching of Scripture because it did not agree with either the conclusions of modern scholars, or what you believed God had been personally revealing to you?

Then you, too, have fallen under the influence of rationalism! As long as we continue to condemn God's Word under our own definitions of acceptance, love, right, good and truth, we convict ourselves beyond any reasonable doubt that we have failed to bear the standard of Scripture.

> Woe *to* those [who are] saying to evil "good," and to good "evil"—putting darkness for light, and light for darkness; putting bitter for sweet, and sweet for bitter. Woe *to* the wise in their own eyes, and—in [the] sight of their own faces—discerning! יְשַׁעְיָהוּ ISAIAH 5:20-21

PART THREE

SUFFICIENT AND SUPREME

A ND IT CAME TO PASS [that] Hezekiah…king of Judah had reigned… and he
did that which *was* right in the eyes
of ADONAI (the LORD)…. He has turned aside the
high places, and broken the standing-pillars in
pieces, and cut down the אֲשֵׁרָה, *'Asherah* [poles],
and beaten down the brass serpent that Moses
made—for up to these days were the sons of Israel burning incense to it—and he called it "a piece
of brass." מְלָכִים ב 2KINGS 18:1-4

The standard that had once saved Israel, the people
now lifted up as a *god*. More than seven hundred years
earlier, Moses had raised up the brass serpent for all Israel to see, so that anyone who "looked expectingly"
toward it would survive the burning serpents' stings.
But in the days before King Hezekiah, the people had
turned the standard into an object of profane worship:
they placed it among the idolatrous high places, pillars
and poles as one of countless venerated things. There
the standard stood—disgraced, obscured, and perverted—nothing more than a useless and defective "piece
of brass." But King Hezekiah, responding to this abom-

inable desecration, "did that which *was* right in the eyes of ADONAI"—he beat down the serpent of brass, crushing it into dust.

In the same way that Hezekiah pulverized that iconic serpent, we too must utterly obliterate the way we—the Body of Messiah—misappropriate and misconstrue the standard of the written Word of God. We have erred by erecting the Scriptures upon a crowded landscape of spiritual and social high places, pillars and poles. We have sinned by reducing the thunderous voice of God's Word to a whisper among a thousand conflicting sounds. Amid the expansive field of a million flying flags, we have lost sight of the standard of Scripture. No longer do men see us lifting up that blessed banner, because we ourselves have no idea where we left it.

As disciples of Messiah, the Scriptures are supposed to be our sole *standard*—something set up high above for all to see—serving as a *tangible* rallying point; a *perceptible* place of focus to which we must "*look expectingly.*" Indeed, it is the only objective authority and guide by which we may reliably find, fix upon, and follow the Master Yeshua (Jesus). But when we lower that superior standard so that it becomes indistinguishable from and intermingled with the banners of men, we inevitably find ourselves swearing allegiance to treasonous, foreign flags. Our focus is drawn away from the standard of Messiah; our eyes, shielded from the brilliance of God's Word.

Like the sons of Israel before us, who hid the standard among a forest of false gods, we are lost: burning incense to our own thoughts, ideas and desires, rather than submitting our will to the Creator and the sufficiency and supremacy of His standard.

THE REALITY OF OUR VULNERABILITY

How did we get here? Why has our stance faltered, our arm weakened, and our eyes wandered? Because we have fraternized with the enemy—colluded with hostile influences—compromised our oath and commitment to uphold the Word of God. Instead of unwaveringly bearing the standard of Scripture, we have listened to other voices—voices that have told us we need the *traditions* of man's customs, interpretations and institutions as Scripture's assistants; voices that say as long as we're doing "good," we can take *expediency's* shortcuts to bypass the Word when it gets in our way; voices that declare the sublime authority of *rationalism*: that when man's reason is in conflict with God's Word, it is not we, but the Scriptures, that are defective.

As we exposed the hostile influences of *tradition, expediency,* and *rationalism*, we witnessed their persuasive and destructive power effectively at work in the real, day-to-day lives of professing believers in Yeshua. We must not be overconfident, however, failing to acknowledge our own susceptibility to their elusive and insidious influence. We must realize that these men and women were not persuaded to reject the guidance of Scripture simply because they had bad *information* or were lacking in *knowledge*. Rather, they themselves opened the door to subversive influences through a breach in their *emotions* and *convictions*. Under similar circumstances—miserable marriages, intense emotional and physical loneliness, the rejection and perceived mistreatment of friends and loved ones—are we so sure we wouldn't make the very same decisions and draw the very same conclusions?

Indeed, in the course of our normal, everyday lives, aren't we relying on **tradition, rather than Scripture**, when we trust government or charitable organizations to meet society's needs? ...or measure our own self-worth by the accumulation of wealth and possessions? ...or look to educational institutions to prepare our children for the future? ...or depend on professional clergy to motivate and direct us concerning God's will for our lives? ...or carry on long-established religious customs, thinking they will make our faith more authentic, or bring us closer to God?

Aren't we following the path of **expediency, rather than Scripture**, when our men work long hours to provide for their households, while neglecting their family's spiritual and emotional needs? ...or our women assume leadership in their homes and congregations under the pretext of men's failure to fulfill their headship roles? …or when we leave it up to congregational youth programs and workers to disciple and spiritually impart to our children? …or we continue doing business with companies that advance immoral causes because we desire to keep consuming their products? …or, in order to appear more relevant, we imitate the world in the hopes of reaching it for Messiah?

And aren't we submitting to the authority of ***rationalism, rather than Scripture***, when we defile ourselves with pornography because we think it's not really adultery? …or abort our unborn children because we think they're not really babies? …or refuse to physically discipline our kids in love because psychologists and sociologists tell us it's harmful to them? …or willfully expose ourselves to questionable or obscene entertainment because we think we're mature enough to handle it? …or fail to confront unbelievers about the consequences of their sin, because we're confident that a loving God would never allow good people to suffer an eternal hell?

Truly, there is no end to the areas and avenues of our lives that are vulnerable to exploitation by hostile influences. Whether in our beliefs, the way we treat our loved ones, how we spend our time, even where we spend our money: moment-by-moment opportunities to compromise the Scriptures abound. None of us are immune to the subliminal seductions of our minds and emotions, which entice us to live independently of God's Word. On the contrary, we are hopeless to overpower the attraction of shortcuts, sidesteps and detours, unless we pledge our lives to bearing the Scriptures alone as God's holy and perfect standard.

UNCONDITIONAL OBEDIENCE

But bearing that standard means far more than simply *recognizing* Scripture as the objective, authoritative, written Word of God. It's even more than *knowing* what the Scriptures say—more than faithfully turning to the Word for comfort, counsel and inspiration. If it is our true intention to renounce the voices we have allowed to influence us—to no longer live only for ourselves, but to follow Yeshua completely and without compromise—then it's time to wake up, and totally commit our lives to God's Word in absolute, unconditional *obedience*. As disciples of Messiah, there is no higher calling than to serve and obey the One and Only Master, whom we love. It is in pursuit of this singular purpose that our ardent ally Mackintosh exhorts us, declaring so eloquently,

> The grand business of the servant is to obey. His object should not be to do a great deal, but simply to do what he is told. This makes all plain; and, moreover, it will make the Bible precious as the depository of the Master's will, to which [the ser-

vant] must continually betake himself to know what he is to do, and how he is to do it. Neither tradition nor expediency [nor rationalism] will do for the servant of Christ. The all-important inquiry is, "What saith the Scriptures." This settles everything. From the decision of the Word of God there must be no appeal. When God speaks, man must bow.

As faithful disciples of Messiah, and humble servants of the God of Israel, our "grand business" before Him is simply *to obey*. We have neither the prerogative *nor the responsibility* to determine our own beliefs, establish our own values, or prescribe our own boundaries for behavior. On the contrary, even though the mere thought of being ordered around makes us squirm in our rebellious skin, our job is no more and no less than to just *do what we're told*.

This, of course, is a slap in the face to our post-modern, Western sensibilities, which tell us to value independence above all, and to define freedom as the license to do as we see fit. But we are, after all, children under the guardianship of a perfect and loving Father. We have to remember that while His Word imposes limits on where we can go and what we can do, His boundless care and abundant provision sets us eternally free! Thank God that He has not left us to fend for ourselves—stranded and forsaken with no map, compass or sustenance—but has endowed us with the completely sufficient "depository of [His] will." Within the confines of Scripture, then, we are free to revel in everlasting safety and truth. It is therefore our responsibility *and joy* to do what it tells us to do, in exactly the way it tells us to do it.

For this reason, whenever we are confronted with life's many alluring alternatives and attractive opportunities—even those that entice us to do "a great deal" for God—there is a principal duty we must perform. As we pause contemplatively at the crossroads of each day's decisions, we are obliged to ask ourselves but a single, simple, quintessential question: *What do the Scriptures say? Which path does the only objective, authoritative, written revelation of God instruct me to take?*

As Mackintosh avows, "This settles everything." In the Scriptures, we have God's will spread out before us —fixed, immutable, and unchangeable. It will not modulate with our moods, accommodate our agendas, or sway with our subjective, spiritual insights. When we are tempted to walk in our flesh away from the truth of God's Word, the Spirit of God actively leads us back to fulfill Scripture's righteous statutes (see Romans 8:4, cf. Ezekiel 36:27, John 16:13). Every thought, theory, assumption, opinion, vision, plan and precept is subject to the judgment of Scripture. Though the Father invites us to draw near to Him for deeper understanding (see Psalm 119:34), we have no such privilege to challenge the wisdom and finality of His rulings. No, "from the decision of the Word there must be no appeal." *What the Scriptures say* is the end of the debate.

As those created in God's very own image, it is our duty *and pleasure* to serve and obey our Master—to voluntarily enslave our minds (see Romans 7:25) and bend our wills to His Word. To be true, *no amount* of the sincerest admiration, respect, veneration, passion or even self-denial is acceptable to God unless it proceeds from our unconditional conformity and unrivaled obedience. Let us not forget "those pungent words of Samuel! *'to obey is better than sacrifice.'*" Indeed, our commitment to the Creator must *far exceed* all adoration and devotion we have for Him. Instead, as the Master Yeshua demonstrated by laying down His life in place of ours, the only adequate expression of love and submission must be displayed through *action*. Whatever the price—no matter the cost—we must heed the admonition of obedience: "When God speaks, man must bow."

THE NARROW PATH

And the price for such obedience is high indeed, because following Yeshua costs us *everything* (Luke 14:33). In exchange for the Ransom paid to redeem our lives from death, we willingly surrender all rights to ourselves; we give up our self-will to do the will of Him who owns us (see Romans 14:8, 1Corinthians 6:19-20). By accepting our salvation and all the rewards and joy that accompany it, we also accept the responsibility to advance His eternally worthy cause. It's an easy yoke (see Matthew 11:28-30) that comes with a hefty price, because choosing to side with God is to both alienate the world and antagonize our former, yet still influential, selves. It is a choice that, in the wake of daily life, can leave us questioning whether the future's everlasting benefits are truly worth today's immediate burdens—whether centering our lives on God is really worth setting aside ourselves. This is the phenomenon that Mackintosh observes when the narrow path of obedience crosses the great plains of opportunity.

> Have we never been tempted as we stood upon the narrow path of obedience, and looked forth upon the golden fields... lying on either side, to exclaim, "Alas! I am sacrificing... for an idea"? Doubtless; but then what if... that "idea" [is] founded upon "Thus saith the Lord"? If so, let us tenaciously hold by it, though ten thousand advocates [oppose us]....

"Doubtless," we have all experienced such temptation. Feeling confined by the boundaries of obedience, we have gazed longingly upon the prolific lives of friends, family, and even strangers. We have envied their successes and accomplishments; we have coveted their full and multifaceted lifestyles. Then, through the resentful eyes of impatience, we have questioned the wisdom of our deepest convictions. *What am I doing, sacrificing myself for words in a Book? Why am I choosing to miss out on life, just to champion an obviously fruitless idea?* "But then," counters Mackintosh, "what if... that 'idea' [is] founded upon 'Thus saith the Lord'?" What if that seemingly lifeless text is really the life-giving Word of God? ...the revelation of our Savior? ...the perfect instructions for a *truly* fruitful life? Has any man in any place at any time ever had an "idea" more worthy of sacrifice? ...more worthy to both live *and die* for?

No! The narrow path of obedience is not laid down on some abstract theory of piety—some idealistic philosophy of righteousness that generates no tangible results or substantial proofs of its ability. On the contrary, obedience is the only avenue that aligns our feeble actions with God's supreme will. It *defines* for us what is right, good, and useful. It *restricts* us to godly thoughts, decisions and behavior. In Yeshua, we are no longer at liberty to choose for ourselves how to use our time, abilities and resources. Instead, we are required to relinquish absolute control to our Master—to permit His Word alone to dictate the direction and actions of our lives. *"What saith the Lord"* is now the limit to which we are bound;

what do the Scriptures say? is the sole standard we are obligated to uphold.

And herein lies a great cost to self, because to hold to such a narrow view of obedience is to invite misunderstanding, ridicule and scorn. Even our own brothers and sisters in Messiah will criticize and dismiss our lives as useless and legalistic when we stand firm on the written Word of God. Many will assert that *if something doesn't directly contradict Scripture, we're allowed to do it. If an action promotes love, peace, and acceptance, we're obliged to do it. If we're all adults and it's (supposedly) not hurting anyone, we're completely and totally free to do it!* But *permissiveness* is not the standard that the Scriptures entreat us to bear—we are not exhorted to test the boundaries of broad-mindedness by going around, through, and behind the back of God's Word. To obey the Scriptures is not to cling unrelentingly to a haphazard set of manmade principals, ethics and laws. Rather, we "tenaciously hold" to the incomparable teaching of Scripture because it is the unmatched, perfect Word of God—wholly deserving of our "narrow-minded" devotion! Mackintosh further encourages us in this.

> It is not by any means a question of obstinate adherence to a man's own notions. Quite the opposite. It is a reverent adherence to the Word of God. Let the reader distinctly mark this. It often happens that, when one is determined, through grace, to

> abide by Scripture, he will be pronounced dogmat-
> ic, intolerant and dictatorial; and, no doubt, one
> has to watch over his temper, spirit, and style, even
> when seeking to abide by the Word of God…. but
> let him reverently bow to the authority of the holy
> Scripture, and he will be looked upon as self-con-
> fident, dogmatic, and narrow-minded. Be it so.

"Be it so," indeed! *Let us be absolutely dogmatic* by insisting that Scripture alone is right, trustworthy, and authoritative. *Let us be utterly intolerant* in the face of fleshly behavior, moral compromise, and unscriptural teaching. *Let us be so completely narrow-minded* when it comes to following the Master Yeshua that we are effec-tively *blind* to all other paths that supposedly lead to God. Seriously—how can we even entertain the alternative? Are we supposed to be *open* to "new" ideas? …or *flexible* in our scriptural convictions? Are we supposed to sanc-tion sin in the name of *tolerance* and the world's definition of "love," just to enable some poor, lost soul's half-heart-ed or self-serving relationship with God? How can any-thing but obeying the Master's commands demonstrate to Him our whole-hearted love and devotion (John 14:21)? How can we as disciples of Messiah justify any-thing *but* narrow-mindedness—single-mindedness—if we hope to successfully adhere to God's Word?

As Mackintosh pictures for us so strikingly, "[It] is better, if it must be so, to stand, like a marble statue, on the pathway of obedience, than to reach the most desirable ends by transgressing the plain precept of the Word of God." We must not move! We must not bend! We must not give way to the influences and temptations that are set against us... to pull, push, and lure us from the straight and level pathway of obedience. At the approach of every opportunity, prospect, and alternative —against the urging of every voice, opinion, and inducement—at the threshold of every sidestep, shortcut, and detour, we must be ready and willing *to stand*... unmovable, unshakable, and, "if it must be so," *alone*. Like the Scriptures themselves, our single-mindedness to uphold the standard of God's Word must also be fixed, immutable and unchangeable. To this path and this path alone, we must dedicate our feet, covenant our eyes, and obligate our hands—to stand upon it as a statue *if we must*, but to nevertheless "tenaciously hold" to it at all costs. It is only by way of the narrow path of obedience that we will discover the truly fruitful life that comes from bearing the standard of Scripture. In this, the Master Himself admonishes us.

> Go in through the narrow gate, because wide *is* the gate and broad the road that is leading to the destruction, and many are those going in through it. How narrow *is* the gate and tight the road that is leading to the life, and few are those finding it!
> מַתִּתְיָהוּ MATTHEW 7:13-14

TIME TO CHOOSE

As disciples of Messiah, this is the very purpose of our lives—the reason we were created and chosen by God. If we are not *bowing our wills* daily to the authority of God's holy and perfect Word—if we are not *standing firm* and walking faithfully upon that pathway of obedience—then we are unqualified for and incapable of raising up Yeshua's banner and leading the way to Life. This is why we must commit our entire existence to the sole cause of bearing the standard of Scripture, because "narrow *is* the gate and tight the road that is leading to the life, and few are those finding it!" Our failure to bear the standard of Scripture is not merely to our own detriment, but to the devastation of both the lukewarm and the lost. The responsibility rests on our shoulders as Yeshua's dedicated disciples to provide a *tangible* rallying point—a *perceptible* place of focus—for those aimlessly wandering the broad road of destruction... to draw their attention and hearts toward the Source of their deliverance. It is up to us to bear the standard of Scripture with our lives—to set the Word of God up high above for all to see—to signal and light the way for others to find, fix upon, and follow the Messiah Yeshua, the only true Way of Life!

So now, we have a decision to make—it is time for us to choose sides. Which will it be? The *broad road*, or the *narrow path?* To do what we *will,* or to do what we're *told?* The *fallibility* of our thoughts, ideas and desires under the influence of hostile forces, or the *infallible instructions* of what the Scriptures say? This is the sobering choice that Mackintosh forces us to face.

> Could the mind of God have devised, or His finger sketched an imperfect chart? Impossible. We must either deny the divinity or admit the sufficiency of *The Book.* We are absolutely shut up to this alternative. There is not so much as a single point between these two positions. If the book is incomplete, it cannot be of God; if it be of God, it must be perfect.

For those of us who have received and accepted Yeshua's salvation, this is *the* defining choice of our lives. We must either openly and defiantly deny that Scripture is the true, perfect Word of God, or we must confess with the full force of our being that the Scriptures are the entirely sufficient, completely supreme standard for life in Messiah.

There is no gray area, here—no wiggle room whatsoever. "There is not so much as a single point between these two positions." It is as extreme a difference as between light and darkness, right and wrong, true and false, good and evil, life and death. Either the Scriptures are God's complete and flawless Word to humanity, or they are a bogus assortment of fairy tales and fabrications. Either the Scriptures are all-sufficient in their guidance and all-supreme in their authority, or they are just a hodgepodge of religious and moral codes scrawled by delusional, feeble-minded fanatics. "If the book is incomplete, it cannot be of God," and any hope you have in life is based on nothing but lies, fantasies, and wishful thinking. But "if [the book] be of God, it must be perfect," thereby placing into your hands the only reliable, authoritative, trustworthy standard to faithfully lead you to the Master. These are the only two options: the Scriptures are either *defective and deficient*, or *sufficient and supreme*…

Which side do you choose?

On the one hand, if you choose *defective and deficient*, you can still live a life full of worship and devotion—it will just be in service to and adoration of a *god* made in *your* image. When the Word is in conflict with your deepest convictions, you will simply edit or twist it until it's in line with your beliefs. When you feel that the Holy Spirit has given you personal revelation or guidance, you will receive it as you deem fit, and not subject it to the rigorous test of Scripture. You will seek out the counsel and advice of other believers, but you will only heed it if it's what you want to hear. You may have a consuming appetite for spiritual books and teachings, but you will starve yourself by compartmentalizing the Scriptures in your everyday life, so that you will never be truly challenged to change.

If, on the other hand, you choose *sufficient and supreme*, you are voluntarily enlisting in the service of God's eternal cause—obligating yourself to bear that high, holy standard *with your life*. When the Word is in conflict with your deepest convictions, you will bow, surrender, and ultimately *annihilate* your self-will. When you feel that the Holy Spirit has given you personal revelation or guidance, you will subject it to the rigorous test of Scripture, and recant your thinking, should you prove to be mistaken. You will seek out the counsel and advice of other believers to hold you accountable to the standard of Scripture, and you will heed it *especially* when it's hard to hear. You will have a consuming appetite not for more spiritual books and teachings, but for the pure, perfect Word of God, so that *His* standard will overtake your everyday life, and you will gladly accept the challenge to change.

Bearing the standard of Scripture requires more than just the *belief* that it provides all the guidance we need, and has the ultimate authority to lead us. No, bearing the standard also demands that we *live out* the implications of that belief. This means willfully subjecting *all* our thoughts, interests and actions to the *supreme* authority of the Word of God. It means setting aside *all* our feelings and preconceptions, and accepting that Scripture alone is *sufficient* to establish our values, determine our beliefs, and dictate the boundaries of our behavior. It means actively resisting and overcoming influences that are hostile to Scripture by bolstering and lifting up that standard with our unyielding obedience. To bear the standard of Scripture, then, is to *stand up*, *stand out*, and *stand strong* for the sake of God's Word at the expense of our own embarrassment, inconvenience, discomfort, loneliness, discrimination, persecution, and even our very lives.

Think about it: if we do not all agree that the Scriptures *alone* constitute the revealed Word of God, how, then, can we say that any two of us are even keeping the same faith? If we do not unite under the banner of Scripture as the sole standard for finding, fixing upon, and following our Master, what makes us think that you and I are even confessing the same Yeshua? …or worshipping the same God? Granted, two people can be *inspired* by the same Scripture in different ways, and, certainly, there is room for some amount of diversity in expressions of faith and life-*style*—but our life-*standard* must be *identical*. The fixed meaning of the text will *never* change, and neither may our conformity to the Word. Unless it is our secret desire to pursue and promote a deity fashioned by our own self-serving interests and graven imaginations, then there really is only one choice before us—one narrow gate to enter, one tight road to travel.

Wake up, disciple of Messiah! If we are *truly* committed to following Yeshua with our lives, then *we have no choice* but to proclaim God's Word by bearing the standard of Scripture—by bowing our wills to it daily—by standing firm in our obedience to do what it says—by lifting it up and championing it over all other voices, standards and ideas—by crying out with the convictions of our mouths, and broadcasting with the actions of our lives, "Scripture alone is the perfect Word of God! It is all-sufficient and supreme! There is no other influence under which we may fall—no other banner worthy of our allegiance!" It is to this singular alternative that we must be "absolutely shut up" in our hearts, minds and deeds. It is for this cause alone that the banner of our life must wave, setting high above for all to see the one and only *choice* that leads to *life*.

> For very near to you is the word (הַדָּבָר, *haDavar*), in your mouth, and in your heart—to do it. See, I have set before you today life and good, [and] death and evil, in that I am commanding you today to love ADONAI (the LORD) your God, to walk in His ways, and to keep His commands…. [L]ife and death I have set before you, [so] choose life, so that you will live, you and your seed, to love ADONAI your God, to listen to His voice, and to cling to Him—for He *is* your life, and the length of your days…. דְּבָרִים DEUTERONOMY 30:14-20

RAISING THE STANDARD

I T IS TIME TO PICK A SIDE—so which will it be? Will we *do* the Word and *listen* to the Voice that is so *near to us* that it is even *in our mouths and our hearts?* Or will we forsake and despise that heavenly sound, growing cold in our love toward God, and loving instead the deities and religions of our own, individual invention?

Today, as a generation of believers in Yeshua, we are failing to make the right choice. We are heading down the same path as those ancient kings of Israel who did evil in the sight of God—who led the people away from following the commands of God—who buried His Word deep beneath the vile wickedness and adulterous perversion of their idolatry. But as it was in the days of good King Josiah, now is the time for us to choose the path of reformation—to unearth and raise up the Scriptures from the rubble of unrighteousness. We would do well to follow the lead of *that* faithful king, who, upon finding the Book that had literally been lost to Israel for generations,

> ...tore his garments... saying, "...[G]reat indeed must be the wrath of ADONAI (the LORD) that has been kindled against us, because our fathers did not obey the words of this book [of the תּוֹרָה, *Torah*] to do all that has been prescribed for us...." And the king went up to the House of ADONAI [with] all the people, from small to great, and he read in their ears all the words of the Book of the Covenant that was found in the House of ADONAI. And the king stood by the pillar, and made the covenant before ADONAI, to walk after ADONAI, to keep His commands, and His testimonies, and His statutes, with all the heart, and with all the soul, to establish the words of this covenant that are written in this Book. And all the people [took their] stand in the covenant. מְלָכִים ב 2KINGS 22:11-23:3

Reeling from the revelation of his and his forbearers' sin, King Josiah tore his garments in piercing grief and shame. Once again, Israel had lost sight of the standard—"the Book of the Covenant"—and summoned the reinfestation of forbidden, foreign gods. Yet, in the most heartbreaking and ironic twist of all, the Book had not merely been cast aside and forgotten, but abandoned among the ruins of God's very own House—lost literally under Israel's feet. For the first time in his life, Josiah heard the pure and perfect Word of God—the Word to which he had always been so near, yet was utterly and inexcusably unaware.

But in that moment of destiny, as he held the newly found Book in his hands, Josiah was compelled to restore the Word to its high and rightful place in the sight of the people of God. He resolutely bore that standard, carried it up to the House of God, then broadcast that rediscovered Word to the ears of all the people. "And the king stood… to establish the words… written in [the] Book. And all the people [took their] stand in the covenant." By *standing up* for the written Word of God, Josiah rallied the people to God's standard. By leading the people back to the authority of Scripture, they, in turn, took the same, bold stand.

Shall we ignore the call to recover the Word we have trampled under our own feet? Will we fail to excavate the Scriptures we have entombed in our own traditions, expediencies and rationalisms? Like King Josiah before us, we are obligated to respond to the revelation of the Word with radical, immediate allegiance. We, too, must take our stand. We, too, must choose the right side. Like Josiah, we need to follow the path of reformation back to the beginning—back to Moses standing at the foot of Mount Sinai—where the Book was first held, and the Word was first read aloud, "and all the people answered [with] one voice, and said, 'All the words which ADONAI has spoken, we will do!'" (Exodus 24:3).

This must be our supreme and sufficient response! Indeed, this is the very *meaning* of our lives. "[T]o love ADONAI your God, to listen to His voice, and to cling to Him"—to stand before a holy God, to hear His glorious and perfect Word, and to respond by pledging our lives only to *do* and *declare* everything He says. Can we truly justify any other response? Could another answer adequately demonstrate the depth of our commitment?

The Master teaches us,

> Everyone who is coming to Me, and is hearing My words, and is doing them, I will show you to whom he is like: he is likened to a man building a house, who dug, and deepened, and laid a foundation upon the rock, and a flood having come, the stream broke forth upon that house, and was not able to shake it, for it has been founded upon the rock. But he who heard [My word] and did not [do

> it], is likened to a man having built a house on the
> ground, without a foundation, against which the
> stream broke forth, and immediately it fell, and
> the ruin of that house became great. LUKE 6:47-49

Unless we dedicate our lives to doing what the Word says, we are nothing but a fallen house that has come to ruin. We are hopelessly unstable without that flawless foundation; tossed about by every torrent and stream. But when we stake our lives on *doing* the Word of God, we are founded on an unmovable, unshakable Rock. We have *the only* reliable footing upon which to stand and lift up a standard for others to fix upon, so that they too can make their way to solid ground.

Our collective sin of repudiating the Word of God has eaten away at our foundation, but if we choose today to *stand up* and *stand out* for the Book, we can unbury that lost treasure, and restore our House to its former glory. If we are truly Messiah's, then we are the ones He expects to have "dug, and deepened, and laid a foundation upon the rock" by doing His Word. Instead, we continually alter and ignore our instructions, and then presume that the structure we are building is sound. This is not our eternal purpose! This is not the destiny we are called to answer! No, we exist "to walk in His ways, and to keep His commands"—to proclaim with everything we are and everything we have, "All the words which ADONAI has spoken, we will do!"

Now is the time to take our stand for the sufficiency and supremacy of Scripture. It is time to give ourselves over without reservation to "listen to His voice" and do only what He says—it is time to put our trust into action, and outwardly demonstrate our inward commitment to the authority of the Word of God. With "one voice," let us declare our devotion, dedicating ourselves to this awesome and singular cause. The time to mourn what was lost has passed—now rejoice! for the perfect Word is found.

> In Your statutes I delight myself;
>> I do not forget **Your word**.
> Deal bountifully with Your servant;
>> I live, and I keep **Your word**.
> My soul has cleaved to the dust;
>> revive me according to **Your word**.
> My soul has dropped from affliction;
>> establish me according to **Your word**.
>
> And I answer him who is taunting me,
>> for I have trusted in **Your word**.
> You did good with Your servant, O ADONAI,
>> according to **Your word**.
> My soul has been consumed for Your salvation;
>> I have hoped for **Your word**.
> From every evil path I restrained my feet,
>> so that I [will] keep **Your word**.
>
> To the age, O ADONAI,
>> **Your word** is set up in the heavens.
> A lamp to my foot *is* **Your word**,
>> and a light to my path.

The unfolding of **Your words** enlighten,
giving understanding [to] the simple.
The sum of **Your word** *is* truth, and to the age
is every judgment of Your righteousness!

תְּהִלִּם PSALMS 119:16,17,25,28; 119:42,65,81,101; 119:89,105,130,160

A CALL TO ACTION

Since the beginning, *the Word* of God has been continually speaking to all creation. In Yeshua, *the Word* became flesh, to demonstrate and proclaim to us the reality of God. But in the Scriptures, the encoded archive of
that very same Word, God continues to speak to us of His
reality and truth, so that we in turn may demonstrate and
proclaim His salvation to the world. The Master Yeshua
upheld Scripture as a standard, not simply because it
speaks of Him, but because Scripture itself *is* His very
Word. When we read and believe that the Scriptures are
true, the will and reality of God are within our reach—
when we uphold God's *standard*, God *Himself* becomes
visible and real to us, as we "look expectingly" toward
that upraised standard, and experience the restoration,
reconciliation and revival of our lives.

If we are to have any hope of fulfilling our call as
Yeshua's disciples—to be pleasing children of our heavenly Father—then we must no longer be satisfied to
merely *profess* our devotion to God. Following Yeshua

requires far more than just the *belief* that Scripture provides all the guidance we need, and the *trust* that it has the ultimate authority to lead us. Being a disciple of Messiah demands that we put into practice and wholeheartedly *live out* the implications of that trust and belief.

> *Have you been demonstrating in your walk with Yeshua that the Scriptures are the sufficient and supreme guide for your daily life?*

> *Have you truly accepted the Scriptures as the ultimate and final standard for determining your values, beliefs and behavior?*

> *Have you unknowingly fallen victim to the hostile influences of tradition, expediency, and rationalism, and been persuaded to undermine, bypass and ignore what the Scriptures say?*

If it is truly your desire to live a life that is completely sold-out to Yeshua—a life of righteousness, selflessness, and service to the Master—then you must dedicate every breath of your being to bearing the standard. In your everyday life, as well as within your sphere of influence, you must *demonstrate* a radical commitment to God, and *take action* according to the matchless direction of His Word.

1 Are you dedicated to bearing the standard? Then **you must admit the sufficiency and supremacy of Scripture**. You must come to the point of conviction that God's Word is enough to lead you through life—you must accept the truth that it deserves your submission, and is worthy of your allegiance. *"[L]ife and death I have set before you, [so] choose life, so that you will live, you and your seed, to love Adonai your God, to listen to His voice, and to cling to Him…" (Deuteronomy 30:19-20)*. Do you trust God with your life? Do you rely upon Him for your care and protection? Then you must permit *His Word alone* to establish your values, *His Word alone* to determine your beliefs, and *His Word alone* to dictate the boundaries of your behavior. Walking each day by the Spirit, Scripture *must in every way* be the supreme, objective guide by which you find, fix upon, and follow the Master Yeshua.

2 Are you dedicated to bearing the standard? Then **you must pledge your life to do what the Scriptures say** —to hear and obey God's Word. *"[A]nd all the people answered [with] one voice, and said, 'All the words which Adonai has spoken, we will do!'" (Exodus 24:3)*. The salvation that the Master bought at such a heavy price cries out for your covenantal response. Answer Him by confirming the commitment of your heart with the confession of your mouth, and obligating yourself to live according to His every Word. *Declare* your dedication to adhere to His instructions; *proclaim* as the purpose of your life to do as He commands. Tell the Master that, "if it must be so," you are willing to endure loneliness, apparent fruitlessness, and all manner of hardship and persecution, should these be the cost of living for Him and faithfully fulfilling His Word.

Are you dedicated to bearing the standard? Then **you must deny yourself, and submit your will, to the full authority of Scripture.** *"[A]nd He died for all, [so] that those living will no longer live for themselves, but for Him who died for them, and was raised again" (2Corinthians 5:15).* As a disciple of Messiah, your life is not your own —the narrow path of service and obedience demands that you make yourself nothing (see Philippians 2:5-7), even hate your own life (Luke 14:26), and readily give up every single thing you have to follow the Master Yeshua (Luke 14:33). But to relinquish that kind of control, you first have to set aside all feelings and preconceptions about what you *want* the Scriptures to say. To deny yourself and submit your will is to do far more than just subject your thoughts and actions to the commands of Scripture—it means surrendering even your *interests, dreams, preferences, and priorities* to the supreme authority of God's perfect Word.

Are you dedicated to bearing the standard? Then **you must read *and know* the Scriptures**. You need to regularly consult and be nourished by God's Word, so that you can recognize the difference between what the Scriptures *actually* say, and what people *think* they mean. *"And Yeshua, answering, said to them, 'You go astray, not knowing the Scriptures, nor the power of God! [D]id you not read that which was spoken to you by God…?'" (Matthew 22:29-31).* As a trustee of God's Word, it is your duty to guard against the misuse and neglect of Scripture—to not pick and choose the verses that you like at the expense of those you don't; to not defend and advance denominational doctrines as if they are more than the mere words of men; to not twist or overlook Scripture in support of a questionable act or belief; to not assume that what you recall of Scripture—or what you've been taught—is actually true to the written revelation of God. When Scripture's plain sense makes sense, seek no other sense. In all ways and at all times, you must pursue the answer to the "all-important inquiry," *what do the Scriptures say?* Above all other voices, opinions, precepts and presumptions, you must know the Word of God for yourself.

Are you dedicated to bearing the standard? Then **you must challenge and resist the influences that are hostile to Scripture**—you must avoid and expose the misleading ways of tradition, expediency and rationalism. *"From every evil path I restrained my feet, so that I [will] keep Your word; From Your judgments I turned not aside, for You—You have directed me" (Psalm 119:101-102).* You need to wake up to the reality that you are under constant bombardment, both from others and from within yourself, to usurp and undermine God's authority in your life. You have to start thinking about and deliberately interrupting the voices you have allowed to influence you. Shut down every thought that elevates personal experience, judgment, and reason above God's Word. Call out compromise that assumes God-pleasing means to justify self-seeking ends. Challenge—and, if you must, escape—religious institutions that are distracted by tradition, or trust tradition (or expediency, or rationalism!) as the gatekeeper and guardian of Scripture. Both within the Body of Messiah, as well as society in general, you must actively confront and engage the culture. *Yours* must be the voice that champions Truth, identifies hostile influences, and provokes others to turn and awaken to the Word.

Are you dedicated to bearing the standard? Then **you must change the way you spend your time, finances, and resources to align with the values of Scripture**. *"Treasure not up to yourselves treasures [here] on the earth... but treasure up to yourselves treasures in heaven... for where your treasure is, there will be also your heart"* (Matthew 6:19-21). Are you filling up your time with entertainment, sports, your job, the internet, or various social and personal interests—including religious activities and events? Are you spending the money entrusted to you by God to pursue those interests, or to maintain a lifestyle in keeping with the world, or to patronize companies that push immoral social agendas because you just can't do without their products, or to support congregations and ministries that purport to build the kingdom of God but in reality are building the kingdoms of men? Are you expending so much of yourself keeping busy and doing things—even "good" things—that you have no physical, mental or emotional reserves available for maintaining deep, committed relationships with others in the Body of Messiah? The way you use your time, finances, and resources—that is, your energy, abilities, home and possessions—exactly reflects what you think is important. You have to start spending, giving, *and even withholding* what you have with greater discernment—you need to look to Scripture to set those limits for you.

Are you dedicated to bearing the standard? Then **you must establish Scripture as the foundation — and Messiah the goal — of all your relationships**; you must covenant with Yeshua-believing family and friends to hold one another accountable to the Scriptures. *"And I call upon you, brothers, through the name of our Master Yeshua, Messiah, that you will all say the same thing, and there will not be divisions among you, and you will be perfectly united in the same mind, and in the same judgment"* (1Corinthians 1:10). It's not enough to base your relationships on common interests, compatible personalities, or even doctrinal perspectives. These things are subject to change over time, and cannot lay the groundwork for a relationship that advances the kingdom of God. Instead, you must sit down and explicitly confirm with your family and friends that Scripture has the first and last word in all your relationships. Make sure that you share the same dedication to following God's Word, and are committed to working through the Scriptures together whenever you have differences. Submit yourselves to one another (see Ephesians 5:21), and pledge to be answerable to rebuke and correction should the need arise. Be prepared to challenge, avoid, and even let go of relationships (see Matthew 10:34-39) that are not governed by the authority of the Word.

Are you dedicated to bearing the standard? Then **you must confront sin and admonish fleshly attitudes and behavior that are opposed to the standard of Scripture**—you must call to account your family and friends in the Body to conform to the Word of God. *"Brothers, if any among you goes astray from the truth, [he who turns] back a sinner from the straying of his way will save a soul from death—and will cover a great number of sins"* (*James 5:19-20*). In a relationship that is governed by the authority of the Word, you not only have the *place*, but the *obligation* to confront all manner of sin. The goal is not to compel or manipulate others into conforming to your personal ideals, but to foster a collective conformity of thought and action to the singular standard of Scripture. Though confrontation can often appear "unloving" by worldly standards—even to the point of your being rejected, or called judgmental and self-righteous—it actually demonstrates a severe *lack* of love to shy away from conflict that results from sin (see Matthew 18:15-20, 1Peter 4:8). Don't evade your responsibility to address sin in the life of a believing family member or friend, but seek to help carry his burdens—not only in a spirit of righteousness, but with sincere humility over your own shortcomings (see Galatians 6:1-2). To call a brother to account may require you to significantly commit of your own time and resources to walk through his restoration together; but you must also be prepared to "put away the evil [person] from among yourselves," and refuse to allow unrepentant sin to remain (see 1Corinthians 5:9-13), should the Word of God be denied.

Are you dedicated to bearing the standard? Then **you must seek out and endeavor to share your daily life with others who are committed to the Scriptures**— you must live your normal, everyday life *interdependently* with other believers in Yeshua. *"The two are better than the one… for if they fall, the one raises up his companion—but woe to the one who falls, and there is not a second to raise him up!" (Ecclesiastes 4:9-10).* Contrary to everything that has been ingrained in you, being the Body of Messiah does not mean living a life of independence and self-sufficiency, punctuated by regular attendance of religious meetings. As a disciple of Messiah, and a unique part of His Body, you are supposed to live as a viable, active member of a *spiritual, intergenerational, extended family.* This means that it is your personal responsibility—not the responsibility of professional clergy, or appointed lay leaders, but *yours*—to strengthen and build up the Body of Messiah. You must be the one who is readily available to encourage, exhort, and demonstrate real love toward others; to live transparently with the goal of duplicating yourself— Yeshua in you—in both natural and spiritual descendants (that is, to make disciples); to rely upon the help and resources of others, as you in turn share everything you have with them (see Acts 2:42-47; 4:32); to facilitate the gathering together of yourself with other Yeshua-believers in order to "provoke one another to love and to good action" (Hebrews 10:24-25). You must open up and share your life with other committed believers in Yeshua—simply, directly, *and often*—not only for your own edification, but for the healthy functioning of Messiah's Body, and as a witness to the power of His Word.

Finally, are you dedicated to bearing the standard? Then **you must put your dedication into action, and live your life as a sold-out Standard Bearer for the Scriptures.** Not only must you end your own unholy alliances with the world, but you must champion the Word as the only legitimate standard for a life that has been reconciled to God. The Master, speaking to the Father, said of us, *"I have given to them Your Word, and the world hated them, because they are not of the world, as I am not of the world; I do not ask that You will take them out of the world, but that You will keep them out of the evil. They are not of the world, as I am not of the world. Set them apart in Your truth—Your Word is truth"* (John 17:14-17). As Yeshua's Standard Bearer, you must remain set apart from the world for the sole sake of saving it. Against every assailing force driving you to concede and bend—

pushing you to conform to its estimation of love, justice, tolerance and truth—*it is time to take your stand....*

You must *stand firm!* on the foundation of the Word —intolerant, dogmatic, narrow-minded and blind—immovable "like a marble statue" in the face of every hostile influence that attempts to tear you down from the solid Rock of God.

You must *stand up!* on the pathway of obedience, and relentlessly advance the glorious banner of Scripture— "tenaciously hold[ing]" that magnificent ensign in your grasp—and uplifting it all the more in the presence of immorality, compromise, and sin.

And you must *stand out!* in the field of the world from both the lost and the lukewarm—drawing attention to that unfurled Flag, and setting your own heart, your comfort, your reputation, and even your well-being in harm's way—as you signal the one, true Way toward truth, freedom and fullness of Life in the Master.

As disciples of Messiah, the solemn charge of bearing the standard has been entrusted to us—to boldly set apart the perfect standard of Scripture, and make it clearly distinguishable from the banners of men. By lifting up Scripture as sufficient and supreme, we are, in effect, lifting up "the Son of Man... [so] that everyone who is believing in Him may have life age-enduring" (John 3:14-15). It is our holy duty to provide that *tangible* rallying point—that *perceptible* place of focus—to draw all attentions and hearts to the One who is bringing our salvation. We must, therefore, raise up our arms, lift up our gaze, and set our sights on the only standard worthy of our allegiance. We must uphold that awesome standard—lifting it high above for all to see—so that everyone, everywhere may "look expectingly," and find, fix upon, and follow the Messiah Yeshua, our King!

ARISE, AND GO FORTH!

The Master is calling us—His Standard Bearers— to rise up and champion His most crucial cause. Especially in these rapidly degenerating times, we must rally together under the same banner for both the prospect of safety, as well as the promise of success. Our gracious God has granted us an inestimable gift, in that He has not left us directionless and alone. He has given us His very Word to cling to—the careful guidance, and faithful instructions of our Maker. If there is any hope in the world of meeting the unimaginable trials that surely lie ahead, then we as Messiah's Standard Bearers must lead the Way—together, we must walk the same path, speak the same Word, and bear the same standard.

It is to this end that I join with my departed compatriot, Mackintosh, as he articulates the sincerest yearning of our kindred spirit. For, indeed,

> we are most anxious that the... reader should rise up from the perusal of this volume with a deepened

sense of the preciousness of his Bible. We earnestly desire that the words, *"The Bible: its sufficiency and supremacy,"* should be engraved, in deep and broad characters, upon the tablet of the reader's heart.... We press upon our readers earnestly to set a higher value than ever upon the Holy Scriptures, and to warn them, in most urgent terms, against every influence, whether of tradition, expediency, or rationalism, which might tend to shake their confidence in those heavenly oracles. There is a spirit abroad, and there are principles at work, which make it imperative upon us to keep close to Scripture—to treasure it in our hearts— and to submit to its holy authority. May God... the Author of the Bible, produce, in the writer and reader of these lines, a more ardent love for that Bible! May He enlarge our experience and acquaintance with its contents, and lead us into more complete subjection to its teachings in all things, that God may be more glorified in us....

Can we do any less in response to God's glorious, life-giving Book than to surrender our wills to its supreme authority? What more can we possibly do or desire than to fully trust in Scripture's absolute sufficiency for answering our every need? This is the conviction that must burn in our minds—the confession that must be cut deep in our hearts. God's Word alone is the incomparable standard for our lives; let us praise and exalt the Master of all masters—the Creator of all things—

who speaks plainly and personally to those He owns through His divine, holy and perfect Word!

I implore you, my fellow-servant of Messiah: in this hour, *we must not falter!* "There is a spirit abroad, and there are principles at work," both outside *and within* the Body of believers, "which make it imperative upon us to keep close to Scripture—to treasure it in our hearts— and to submit to its holy authority." The whole earth is waiting (and indeed, has long been waiting) for a generation of Standard Bearers that would rise up *as one man* to carry the Master's banner into the fray—to willingly expose ourselves as a forerunner for the people, and as a target for the enemy. For the eternal cause of Messiah, and for the sake of future generations, we must not lie down—*we must not fall back!*—and allow the world's arrogant armies to continue their rebellious and destructive crusade unchallenged. *Not on our watch! This far, and no further!* The time of hesitating between two opinions is done—you must now decide *where* you will make your stand, and *whose standard* you will bear.

> Therefore, [since] we also [are] having so great a cloud of witnesses set around us, having put off every weight and the closely-surrounding sin, through perseverance we must run the race that is set before us, fixing [our eyes] on the author and perfecter of faith—Yeshua—who, over-against the joy set before Him, endured an [execution] stake, [and] having despised [the] shame, also sat down

at the right hand of the throne of God. For consider
again Him who endured such opposition from the
sinners to Himself, [so] that you will not be wea-
ried in your souls—giving up. עִבְרִים HEBREWS 12:1-3

Will you, today, accept the Scriptures' complete authority to govern who you are and what you believe? Will
you pledge at this moment to allow only God's Word to
set your boundaries, establish your priorities, and tell
you how to live your life daily for Yeshua (Jesus)? Will
you join with me in the eternal cause of Messiah to bear
the standard of Scripture, and declare with every breath
of your being the sufficiency and supremacy of His perfect Word? If you are so willing, then you must utterly abandon yourself into the hands of the Living God,
and be "absolutely shut up" in your bones to this single,
sacred purpose. Today, we must fall before ADONAI our
God in unreserved submission, crushed under the realization of our unworthiness to bear both His standard,
and His Name. Then, in perfect humility and obedience,
arise! and take up His Word—and boldly wave that most
brilliant, beaming standard to enlighten every eye with
something most sufficient and supreme to see.

Arise, and go forth, you faithful of Messiah!

Arise, and go forth, you Standard Bearers for God!

May ours be the generation that stands firm on the
sufficiency and supremacy of Scripture. May we be the

ones to stand up, and put that radical belief into revolutionary action. May all our serving and sacrifice be acceptable to You, O God; forgive us for seeking our own way, and embracing the influences that lead us astray. Lift us up in righteousness, Father, as we raise up the banner of Your Son; stabilize our hearts and minds, as we stand boldly on the foundation of Your Word. Fill us with Your Spirit, ADONAI, and give us the strength to walk in Your commands. Cause us, Master, to step only on the perfect path of Your Word, as we rise up, and go forth, and bear the standard of Scripture.

> O God, You cast us off, You broke us—
>   [You] had been angry.
>   Turn back to us!
>
> You have caused the land to tremble,
>   You have broken it.
>   Heal its breaches, for it has moved.
>
> You have shown Your people a hard thing;
>   You have caused us to drink
>   [the] wine of staggering.
>
> [But] You have given to those fearing You
>   a standard to flee to
>   because of truth. Selah.
>
> [So] that Your beloved ones may be rescued,
>   save *with* Your right hand,
>   and answer us!

תְּהִלִּים PSALMS 60:1c-5

ARE YOU DEDICATED TO BEARING THE STANDARD?

JOIN THE CAUSE

MY FELLOW-SERVANT OF MESSIAH, it is time to rise up and dedicate your life to bearing the standard of Scripture!

My heart's desire is that this message has not been merely another intellectual exercise for you, but that it has sparked you to take permanent, radical and immediate action in your life. I truly believe that there is a movement—God willing, a revolution—waiting to begin... indeed, *needing* to begin. Will you join the cause of Messiah and uphold the Scriptures? Will you be a Standard Bearer for Him?

In *Bearing the Standard*, I gave a call to action, and challenged you with ten specific action points (*see p. 135*). Here are a few practical suggestions to help you take that action, and affect a change not only in your own life, but also in the lives of others within your sphere of influence:

First, reread the book. While the message of *Bearing the Standard* is a simple one, I've given you a lot to process here. I know that even for myself, I had to revisit these concepts over and over again before that gradual "renewing of [my] mind" finally took hold. As you reread this book, it will help retrain you to actively challenge your thinking and perceptions, so that you can see more clearly where you (and others) have been led to sidestep, shortcut, and take detours around the Word of God.

Second, give copies of this book away. Become an "inreach evangelist" to the Body of Messiah by giving away copies of this book to every Yeshua-believer you meet—including pastors and congregational leaders, as well as people in their teens, twenties and thirties—telling them how the message of *Bearing the Standard* has affected your life. Visit bearingthestandard.org to learn more about ordering copies of the book at not-for-resale, bulk-rate discounts.

Third, get your family and friends to read this book, and then discuss it with them. After you give your loved ones a copy of this book (or they read the *ebook*, or listen to the *audio book*), go to bearingthestandard.org and download the free discussion guide. The goal here is for *Bearing the Standard* to serve as a tool to help you fulfill the action point of establishing Scripture as the foundation—and Messiah the goal—of all your relationships. By being on the same page, so to speak, you will be able to more effectively build and serve the Master together.

Fourth, log on to bearingthestandard.org for more resources and further equipping. Join the cause, find tools to equip you, and get help for spreading the word about how every faithful follower of Messiah must bear the standard of Scripture.

And finally, take the Standard Bearers' Pledge. The pledge (beginning on the following page), based on the call to action, is meant for one purpose only: to help each of us declare before God, and in the presence of our fellow-servants of Messiah, our intention to bear the standard of Scripture. You may choose to make this a public declaration, or perhaps use it as part of your commitment to bear the standard with your family and friends. Regardless, I pray this pledge will aid you in confirming the commitment of your heart with the confession of your mouth, as you speak forth your dedication to uphold the sufficient and supreme standard of God's holy and perfect Word.

My fellow Standard Bearer for God, don't let the truth of this fundamental message lie fallow within you. Join with me in putting our shared trust into action, and outwardly demonstrating our inward commitment to the authority of the Word of God. With one voice, let us declare our devotion to God and His Word, dedicating ourselves together to the awesome and singular cause of bearing the standard of Scripture.

The Standard Bearers' Pledge

In the sight of the God of Israel, and in the Name of the Master, the Messiah Yeshua (Jesus),

I admit the sufficiency and supremacy of Scripture.

I believe that the Word of God is enough to lead me through life;

and I accept the truth that God's Word deserves my submission, and is worthy of my allegiance.

I will therefore permit

His Word alone to establish my values,

His Word alone to determine my beliefs,

and *His Word alone* to dictate the boundaries of my behavior.

Walking each day by the Spirit, I will allow the Scriptures *in every way* to be the supreme, objective guide by which I

find,

fix upon,

and follow the Master Yeshua (Jesus).

Today, **I pledge my life to do what the Scriptures say**—to hear and obey God's Word.

I dedicate myself to adhere to His instructions;

I proclaim as the purpose of my life to do as He commands;

and, if it must be so, I am willing to endure loneliness, apparent fruitlessness, and all manner of hardship and persecution, should these be the cost of living for God, and faithfully fulfilling His Word.

From this moment on,

I deny myself, and submit my will to the full authority of Scripture.

I set aside all my feelings and preconceptions about what I *want* the Scriptures to say;

and I surrender my interests, dreams, preferences and priorities to the supreme authority of God's perfect Word.

As a Standard Bearer for God,

I will read and *know* the Scriptures;

> **I will challenge and resist the influences that are hostile to God's Word;**

> > and **I will change the way I spend my time, finances, and resources to align with the values of Scripture**.

I will establish Scripture as the foundation—and Messiah the goal—of all my relationships;

> **I will confront sin and admonish fleshly attitudes and behavior that are opposed to the standard of the Word;**

> > and **I will seek out and endeavor to share my daily life with others who are committed to the Scriptures.**

From this day forward, **I will put my dedication into action by living my life as a sold-out Standard Bearer for the Scriptures.**

I will *stand firm!* on the foundation of God's Word;

I will *stand up!* on the pathway of obedience;

and I will *stand out!* in the field of the world for the sake of both the lost and the lukewarm.

May God be accepting of all my serving and sacrifice, causing me to step only on the perfect path of His Word, as I freely and wholeheartedly pledge my life to bearing the standard of Scripture.

ᘓ

REFERENCES

Born Again Adults Less Likely to Co-Habit, Just as Likely to Divorce.
(2001, August 6). Retrieved February 9, 2012 from http://
www.barna.org/barna-update/article/5-barna-update/56-
born-again-adults-less-likely-to-co-habit-just-as-likely-to-
divorce

*Born Again Christians Just As Likely to Divorce As Are Non-
Christians.* (2004, September 8). Retrieved February 7, 2012
from http://www.barna.org/barna-update/article/5-barna-
update/194-born-again-christians-just-as-likely-to-divorce-
as-are-non-christians

Charles, Tyler. (2011, September/October). (Almost) Everyone's
Doing It. *Relevant, 53,* 65-69.

Comstock, Gary David. (1993). *Gay Theology Without Apology.*
Cleveland, OH: Pilgrim Press.

Copen, C., Daniels, K., Vespa, J., Mosher, W. (2012, March 22).
*First Marriages in the United States: Data From the 2006–
2010 National Survey of Family Growth.* Retrieved March 23,
2012 from http://www.cdc.gov/nchs/data/nhsr/nhsr049.pdf

Gay clergy eligible for all Episcopal ministry. (2009, July 15). Retrieved July 6, 2012 from http://www.usatoday.com/ news/religion/2009-07-14-episcopal-church-clergy_N.htm

Jacobs, Mary. (2005, December 10). *Q&A with Chuck Smith Jr.* Retrieved July 11, 2012 from http://www.religionnewsblog. com/14301/qa-with-chuck-smith-jr

Johnson, Luke Timothy. (2007, June 15). *Scripture & Experience.* Retrieved June 13, 2012 from http://commonwealmagazine. org/homosexuality-church-1

Jones, Stanton L. (2006). A Study Guide and Response to: Mel White's What the Bible Says—and Doesn't Say—About Homosexuality. Wheaton, IL: Wheaton College.

Mohler, Albert. (2009, July 16). *The Compassion of Truth: Homosexuality in Biblical Perspective.* Retrieved June 18, 2012 from http://www.albertmohler.com/2009/07/16/the-compassion-of-truth-homosexuality-in-biblical-perspective-2/

Moore, Russell D. (2012, March 15). *Should I Divorce If I'm Miserable?* Retrieved March 18, 2012 from http://www. russellmoore.com/2012/03/15/should-i-divorce-if-im-miserable/

Most Twentysomethings Put Christianity on the Shelf Following Spiritually Active Teen Years. (2006, September 11). Retrieved August 29, 2012 from http://www.barna.org/ teens-next-gen-articles/147-most-twentysomethings-put-christianity-on-the-shelf-following-spiritually-active-teen-years

New Marriage and Divorce Statistics Released. (2008, March 31). Retrieved March 11, 2012 from http://www.barna.org/

barna-update/article/15-familykids/42-new-marriage-and-divorce-statistics-released

Practical Outcomes Replace Biblical Principles As the Moral Standard. (2001, September 10). Retrieved February 8, 2012 from http://www.barna.org/barna-update/article/5-barna-update/58-practical-outcomes-replace-biblical-principles-as-the-moral-standard

Scaramanga, UrL. (2006, January 23). *Brian McLaren on the Homosexual Question: Finding a Pastoral Response.* Retrieved July 12, 2012 from http://www.outofur.com/archives/2006/01/brian_mclaren_o.html

Smid, John. (2011, August 12). *Transitions – Report on TEN [The Evangelical Network] Conference 2010.* Retrieved July 11, 2012 from http://www.gracerivers.com/1982-corvette-2/

Swiatocho, Kris. (2005, September 14). *Missionary Dating: On a Mission to Get Him Saved.* Retrieved May 11, 2012 from http://www.crosswalk.com/family/singles/missionary-dating-on-a-mission-to-get-him-saved-1351350.html?ps=0

ABOUT THE AUTHORS

CHARLES HENRY MACKINTOSH
was born in 1820 in County Wicklow,
Ireland. Following a spiritual experience
when he was eighteen years old, he ultimately gave himself to "the ministry of

the Word" in his mid-twenties, delving heavily into writing
and public speaking. CHM, as he was known, participated in
the great revival in Ireland of 1859 and 1860, and also edited
the periodical *Things New and Old* for twenty-one years.

Mackintosh is most known for his *Notes on the Pentateuch*, which begins with a 334 page volume on Genesis,
and concludes with a two-volume work on Deuteronomy,
spanning more than 800 pages. According to one histori-
an, Mackintosh was "no critical scholar... nevertheless [he]
had a marked gift for simple Biblical exposition, and his
works on the Pentateuch had an enormous vogue as simple
aids to devotional interpretation for the first five books of
the Bible." Seven volumes of his *Miscellaneous Writings* were
also compiled, totaling over 2,500 pages.

Mackintosh was associated with the Plymouth Brethren, a nineteenth century Christian movement that traces
its roots back to Dublin, Ireland. The Brethren were char-
acterized by their ardent adherence to Scripture as the sole
authority for faith and practice, resulting in their avoidance
of many otherwise widely accepted Christian traditions.

Mackintosh died on November 2, 1896, and was buried
next to his beloved wife, Emma, in Cheltenham, England.

 **KEVIN GEOFFREY**, born Kevin Geoffrey Berger, is the firstborn son of a first-generation American, non-religious, Jewish family. Ashamed of his lineage from childhood, he deliberately attempted to hide his identity as a Jew, legally changing his name as a young adult. After experiencing an apparently miraculous healing from an incurable disease, Kevin began to search for God. Eventually, he accepted Yeshua as Messiah, a decision which would ultimately lead him to be restored to his Jewish heritage. Today, Kevin is a strong advocate for the restoration of all Jewish believers in Yeshua to their distinct calling and identity as the faithful remnant of Israel.

In 2006, Kevin was licensed by the IAMCS, and later ordained by Jewish Voice Ministries International. He has been involved in such endeavors as congregational planting, leadership development, and itinerant teaching, but is best known as a writer, having authored seven books to date. In addition to writing about uniquely Messianic Jewish topics, Kevin's clear and impassioned teachings focus on true discipleship, radical life-commitment to Yeshua, and upholding the Scriptures as God's perfect standard.

Kevin is a husband, a father, and also the principal laborer of Perfect Word Ministries, a Messianic Jewish equipping ministry. He currently resides in Phoenix, Arizona, with his wife Esther and their three cherished sons, Isaac, Josiah and Hosea.

Join the cause.
bearingthestandard.org

Other books by Kevin Geoffrey

Being a Disciple of Messiah

Deny Yourself

Messianic Daily Devotional

Messianic Mo'adiym Devotional

Messianic Torah Devotional

The Real Story of Chanukah

For more information visit
perfect-word.org